Vision in Action

PUTTING A WINNING STRATEGY TO WORK

Benjamin B. Tregoe
John W. Zimmerman
Ronald A. Smith
Peter M. Tobia

KEPNER-TREGOE, INC.

A FIRESIDE BOOK
Published by Simon & Schuster Inc.
New York • London • Toronto •
Sydney • Tokyo • Singapore

Fireside

Simon & Schuster Building
Rockefeller Center
1230 Avenue of the Americas
New York, New York 10020

First Fireside Edition, 1990

FIRESIDE and colophon are registered trademarks
of Simon & Schuster Inc.

Designed by Irving Perkins Associates
Manufactured in the United States of America

10 9 8 7 6 5 4 3 2 1
10 9 8 7 6 5 4 3 2 1 Pbk.

Library of Congress Cataloging in Publication Data

Vision in action : putting a winning strategy to work / Benjamin B.
    Tregoe . . . [et al.].
        p.   cm.
    Includes index.
    1. Strategic planning.   2. Strategic planning—Employee
participation.   3. Management—Employee participation.   I.
Tregoe, Benjamin B.
    HD30.28.V56   1989
    658.4′012—dc19   89-31067
                                                            CIP
                                                            r89

ISBN 0–671–68068–4
    0–671–70643–8 Pbk.

F

ACKNOWLEDGMENTS

THIS BOOK WOULD NOT HAVE BEEN POSSIBLE WITHOUT THE CONTRIBUTION and participation of the people we interviewed and the organizations they represent. We have been allowed to "go public" because of their unselfish desire to advance the quality of strategic thought and action in organizations around the world.

The consulting experience of our colleagues at Kepner-Tregoe helped shape our approach to formulating and implementing vision.

In addition, Annette Tobia provided invaluable critiques of the manuscript as it progressed. Charlotte Zimmerman's editorial assistance was of great help. She also provided a safe and sane haven for the innumerable meetings on the book.

Helen Turiano merits special thanks for typing—and retyping—the manuscript.

Contents

Introduction
by Tom Peters

A book on strategy that's practical? That's based a hundred percent on real examples the authors have lived with? That's chock-a-block with quotes from key players in each company involved? That has as many service-company examples as manufacturing examples? That's technically sophisticated, yet not loaded with bubble charts and hopelessly confusing wiring diagrams? That devotes as much time to commitment to strategy and implementation down the line as it does to the formulation process?

The answers to each of those questions is a resounding Yes. To my mind, *Vision in Action* is the first of its kind, a book that does all of the above and yet is manageable in length.

We travel through pitfalls and successes with nineteen organizations, each facing up to today's volatile marketplace conditions. They range from Abilene Christian University and The Federal Reserve Bank of Cleveland to Dow Chemical, Fuji Photo Film and The J. M. Smucker Company. Ben Tregoe, John Zimmerman, Ronald Smith and Peter Tobia take us on a careful journey through the thickets of strategy and implementation. They start (as so few do), not by analyzing "forces at work," but by emphasizing the often-ignored link between strategy and operations; implementation is never a "last chapter" issue in this book.

After the strategy/operations link has been thoroughly explored, the authors run through the process of selecting a

9

Driving Force (one of eight, such as Products Offered, Markets Served or Method of Distribution/Sale). The examination is detailed, but never slips into a jargony presentation; and despite the complexity of the issues addressed, simplicity and common sense are emphasized, not theoretical techniques requiring the services of a pair of Cray supercomputers and a full-time twenty-person strategy department.

Half the book deals with formulating strategy—always, I must underscore, with real examples and assessments by the actual participants. The other half of the book deals with implementation. Once more, simple yet robust schemes are offered—and, once again, real-life examples with rich detail are the data. What distinguishes this book is its mix of formulation and implementation, and the fact that roughly fifty percent of its contents is devoted to analyses by practicing executives. My chief irritation with management literature is that it suffers from the same thing that afflicts our firms—the failure to integrate strategy/purpose/market/customers with operations/implementation/organization/systems/people. *Vision in Action* takes a giant and long overdue step to meet this criticism and, thus, to respond to a critical need.

Authors' Introduction

OVER THE PAST FIVE YEARS, A FLURRY OF BOOKS AND ARTICLES HAVE BEEN written to get organizations moving again. Some tell us that the key to an organization's success lies in the search for excellence; others advise us to imitate the art of Japanese management; still others suggest one-minute solutions to today's difficulties. However divergent the existing approaches have been, they all share a common point of departure: the conviction that today's organizations must be better run. To survive and succeed in a savage, worldwide competitive environment, you must "stick to your knitting," pay attention to the nuts and bolts, do things right.

There is nothing wrong with this advice. In fact, the focus on "excellence" has helped to improve day-to-day operations, the "how-we-do-things" dimension of many of our organizations. But that is not enough. Back in 1983, *Business Week* examined the highly touted "excellent" companies that were featured in Tom Peters and Robert Waterman's best-seller *In Search of Excellence* to determine how well these companies were doing. What *Business Week* found was that however excellent these companies might be, some of them were in serious trouble. In a good number of cases, the difficulty did not stem from operational inadequacies but from strategic deficiencies. These companies were failing because their vision was flawed.

We do not wish to criticize the prevailing wisdom regarding operational excellence. Obviously, being well run is critical to

11

success. But what about being well directed? "Sticking to your knitting" is, after all, good strategic advice. But how do you determine what your "knitting" truly is, or what to do when the yarn runs out? That is also critical to success. The last thing a company headed in the wrong direction needs is to get there more efficiently.

This is a book about the strategic dimension that is so often missing in discussions about how organizations can improve their performance. For us, vision or strategy is about what an organization wants to be in terms of products, markets, and resources or capabilities. In today's uncertain and extremely competitive business environment, continued success depends as much on the quality of strategic thinking—and on how well that thinking becomes imprinted on every decision an organization makes—as it does on the effectiveness of operations.

There are two central and related themes addressed in this book. First, how do you make vision happen? Put differently, how do you take the strategic direction formulated by top management, whether at corporate or business unit level, and translate that direction into reality? To do this requires broad participation down through the organization. Thus, our second theme centers on the question: How do you go about achieving the participation necessary for implementing vision?

This book focuses on strategy implementation, and it offers an organization's view of the subject. You will see real organizations working in "real time" on the issues of implementing vision. And you will be privy to the thinking of executives and managers as they proceed along the continuum from strategy formulation through implementation to action. Since you travel the same path, you will come away with a practical understanding of what the issues are and how to go about resolving them.

Ours is not a theoretical treatment of strategy. While there are sound theoretical underpinnings to our work, we have chosen to focus instead on the practical application of ideas. Since this is a book for those interested in taking strategic action, we have avoided wherever possible presenting diagrams, flow charts, and all the other accoutrements of complexity. Our aim is to rivet attention on how organizations just like yours have struggled to live by a vision of the future and at the same time remain operationally sound.

Participation, our second theme, has become something of a buzzword, but most discussions center on how to improve operating effectiveness through greater employee involvement. Rarely is the subject of participation in the strategy process discussed. This book shows the real power of strategic participation and provides guidance on how that participation can be structured.

For the past fifteen years we have worked with hundreds of organizations all over the world on strategic decision making. Since 1980, much of that work has been directed toward answering the questions: How do you implement vision? How do you make strategic thinking everyone's road map? From our extensive client base, we have selected nineteen organizations whose experiences best illustrate how vision has become a reality for them. *Vision in Action* is their story. It tells how organizations and the people behind them have taken on the challenge to think in visionary terms and to live in terms of their vision. It presents the "aha's" and "oh no's." You can learn from both.

The organizations we will feature range in size from a large multinational chemical company to a small denominational university. They vary in complexity from the typical functional structure to a matrix organization structure and are both profit and nonprofit oriented. They are located in Canada, England, Japan, and the United States. Many of these organizations have not appeared on any of those "excellence" lists published in books and business magazines. Perhaps your organization has not appeared either. These organizations are probably a lot like yours and were selected for that reason. Winning is not just a matter of being well known, but of setting the right direction and then following through to sustain growth and profitability for the shareholders and employees.

The organizations we feature are working quietly on the frontier of strategy innovation. Their executives, managers, and employees are motivated by quarter-by-quarter performance. But they are equally concerned with the longer-term stewardship of the resources entrusted to them. They are involved in the difficult and challenging work of setting and living by a clear vision of the future. This is the surest way to survive and grow in these rapidly changing times.

Every organization has some sense of where it is going, however unarticulated this may be. The organizations here were compelled to consider their strategic direction consciously for a variety of reasons. The OTC Group was making the transition from a family-owned to a professionally managed business, while Huntington Bancshares, Inc., was confronting radical change in its industry. The Fuji Photo Film Company, Ltd., realized that Japan's growth was slowing and operational excellence was not enough, and the J. M. Smucker Company saw that all of its short- and long-range planning could not satisfactorily answer the question "Where should we be headed?"

We have chosen these particular organizations because of the depth of our relationships with them in the strategic process. The idea of writing this book developed well into our work with these organizations. Each of them has reviewed the contents of the book. We have related their experiences as they actually happened, while respecting proprietary information. Here are the organizations you will meet in the pages that follow:

Abilene Christian University: Fourth-largest private university in the southwestern United States, affiliated with the Church of Christ.

Central and South West Corporation: A Dallas, Texas, holding company with four electric utilities in the Southwest.

Consumers Packaging, Inc. (formerly Consumers Glass, Inc.): Canadian producer of glass and plastic packaging.

Courtaulds Fabrics Group (part of the Textiles Group of Courtaulds, PLC, in London, England): A major manufacturer of fabrics for apparel, home furnishings, and industrial applications.

The Dow Chemical Company: Global producer of chemicals, plastics, and pharmaceutical and agricultural products, based in Midland, Michigan.

Dow Corning Corporation: Worldwide developer, manufacturer, and marketer of silicones for a wide variety of applications, located in Midland, Michigan.

The Federal Reserve Bank of Cleveland: One of the twelve regional banks which make up the central bank of the United States.

Fuji Photo Film Company, Ltd., Chemical Paper, In-Company Information System, Electronic Imaging, and Graphic System Divisions: Multinational producer of consumer and commercial film, magnetic tapes, optical products, and the like, with headquarters in Tokyo.

Gund Investment Corporation: A privately held investment company with headquarters in Princeton, New Jersey, offering a wide range of investment and professional management services.

Huntington Bancshares, Inc.: A regional bank holding company operating from Columbus, Ohio, and offering a full range of banking services in nine states.

The J. M. Smucker Company: Manufacturers of branded food products, including jams, ice cream toppings, peanut butter, and industrial fruit for commercial uses, with headquarters in Orrville, Ohio.

Kawasaki Steel Corporation, Steel Business Planning Division: Worldwide manufacturers of flat-rolled steel products with diversification into electronics and urban development, located in Tokyo.

NISSAY (formerly Nippon Life Insurance Company), Group Insurance, Life Insurance, Domestic/Overseas Investments, and Real Estate Divisions: A Japanese life-insurance company, headquartered in Osaka and Tokyo, that has recently expanded internationally.

Oki Electric Industry Company, Ltd., Electronic Devices Group and Quality Reliability Division: Worldwide manufacturer of electronic-switching, data-processing, and applied electronics systems, with headquarters in Tokyo.

OTC Group (formerly Owatonna Tool Company): Located in Owatonna, Minnesota, a division of the SBX Corporation manufacturing automotive special tools and hardware, as well as cams and pumps for industrial applications.

R. P. Foundation Fighting Blindness: A Baltimore, Maryland, foundation engaging in national eye research dedicated to finding a cure for degenerative retinal diseases.

Showa Denko K.K., Plastics Division: Tokyo producers of a wide range of synthetic chemicals, with new ventures in data processing and financial services.

Varity Corporation (formerly Massey-Ferguson, Ltd.): A Toronto-based international manufacturer of farm and industrial machinery, diesel engines, and automotive and hydraulic components.

Washington Mutual Financial Group (formerly the Washington Mutual Savings Bank): An organization offering a wide range of banking and related services, including retail and commercial banking, with headquarters in Seattle, Washington.

To prepare for this book, in-depth interviews were conducted with a cross section of people in each of the participating organizations. Appendix A provides the names and titles of all the executives of these organizations whom we quote, along with a more detailed description of their organizations. Space limitations and repetition prohibit us from quoting all those interviewed. What we will add to the interviews from our consulting experience are the major concepts and approaches to implementing strategy that apply to any organization.

As a facilitator and a partner to their efforts to make strategy a reality, our role has been to steer the thinking process of the people involved. We do not prescribe. We bring a questioning approach and a thinking process to an organization. These enable executives and managers throughout that organization to dig out and put into perspective the kinds of information, feelings, and intuition that lead them to develop their organization's vision and then go about the task of bringing that vision to life. No one can do it for them—or for you!

Although this is a book about implementation, we also include a discussion of strategy formulation. It is essential to understand what makes a clear statement of strategy before we can talk meaningfully about how to implement it. Getting the vision out to make it clear is the first step on the continuum that leads from vision to action.

In writing *Vision in Action,* we have avoided the cumbersome "he or she" reference and instead use the masculine personal pronoun. Convenience and not male chauvinism dictated this usage.

The book follows the flow of the two themes mentioned earlier. The first, how to make vision happen, is covered in the first four chapters. Chapter 1 deals with the relationship between strategy and operations. To make vision a reality, you must understand why operational effort can cripple strategic thought and action. Chapter 2 focuses on defining what clear vision is and knowing when you have one. Chapter 3 discusses how to link your strategic conclusions to long-range planning, annual budgeting, and day-to-day operations. Chapter 4 deals with sustaining strategy over time. This includes understanding and acting upon the implications of strategy for organization structure, culture and beliefs, monitoring and information systems, critical issues, and review and update. We call these the vital signs for strategic success.

The second theme of the book zeros in on achieving participation to make vision happen. Developing the broad, yet defined, participation required to make strategy work is the subject of Chapter 5. One of the essential ingredients for strategic participation is the effective communication of vision down through the organization. This is the topic for Chapter 6. Finally, in Chapter 7 we take a reflective look at the experiences of the organizations we have worked with and ask: What are the remaining challenges in implementing vision? We look at where these organizations have run into trouble with strategic decision making and then outline corrective actions.

Knowing how to make strategy work requires understanding and action at many levels throughout an organization. While there have been a number of books and articles written about strategic thinking, most, if not all, are written for narrow audiences, such as senior executives, planners, or marketers. Our view of the reach of strategic thinking or vision is far wider. It is for executives in the boardroom, senior managers, middle managers, key individual contributors, supervisors and employees, field sales personnel, and staff and administrative support groups. All must understand, share in, and contribute to the organization's vision, or that vision will not become a reality.

"When there is no vision, the people perish."* And so do their organizations. But for vision to be understood, shared,

* *Proverbs*, xxix, 18

and put into action, a conscious approach or thinking process is required. This book tells how to develop that conscious approach to vision and how to gain the breadth of participation to make it work. The collective experiences of the organizations you will meet in the pages that follow will provide practical insights and a powerful process for setting the future vision or direction of your own organization and for making that vision come to life.

CHAPTER I
Strategy versus Operations

VISION UNDER FIRE

Vision takes nurturing. This message comes through from just about every organization we have worked with. Vision dies when it is left untended, or when it fails to touch every major aspect of operations from people to systems. Operational pressures are just too intense. They easily overwhelm strategic vision. We begin here by having our organizations share their practical insights.

Why is there such a precarious balance between vision and operations? Why is strategy so fragile?

PETER AUBUSSON: At the Courtaulds Fabrics Group, we spent great effort to get our mid-level managers to think strategically about their end of the business. There was quite a lot of skepticism because our middle managers hadn't been expected to think strategically before. We had been through a difficult few years, and managers had been told they either lived or died by the quarterly success of their operations. Now, to get these people to look more toward the long term was quite difficult at first.

Is the problem that people don't know how to think strategically, or that operational pressures inhibit such thinking?

DALE JOHNSON: Both are true. Historically, at the OTC Group, most of our time—from my position as president right on down—was invested in operations. We were concerned with such issues as cost allocation, response time, and predictability of demand. There is nothing wrong with paying attention to operations, but we also must be mindful of directional issues.

We lacked a process to set strategy. Our company was changing from a small, entrepreneurial, family-owned business to a large, professionally run operation. There were differences of opinion among family members. We didn't share a common vision of where we were going, and we were not sure how to proceed.

Why do we seem "stuck" with a short-term operational perspective?

FRANK WOBST: We must educate people to think strategically. Historically, at Huntington Bancshares and in our industry, we have adopted a short-term orientation. This is particularly true of publicly held companies. When we're talking about competing with the Europeans or the Japanese, it is almost impossible to succeed with this abbreviated time perspective. To preserve the long-term, strategic well-being of an organization, the board of directors and the management must go beyond the quarter-by-quarter, operational outlook.

Can operational decisions become the direction by default?

BILL TEAGUE: That question brings to mind an incident that took place not at Abilene Christian University but at a company that manufactured household cleaning products, where I once worked. We had excess production capacity. We started manufacturing bar soap to be used in motels, with the name of the hotel imprinted on each bar. Our profit margin on this item was small, but at least we used some of that capacity.

Things began to change. Our branded products became increasingly accepted in the marketplace. Production went up, and we had to work overtime. We began to lose margin because of higher labor costs. After six months someone finally asked, "Why are we producing soap for hotels? That was never meant to be a *major* part of our business."

LARRY STORDAHL: Without a clear sense of direction at the OTC Group, things were done which just didn't fit strategically. During the seventies, we bought a large paint system with the capabilities we wanted but more capacity than we needed for ourselves. The purchase cost was significant, and so, driven by financial considerations, we wound up selling paint services to outside customers. This was a significant departure from our traditional customer base and product line. Because the paint company that evolved was operationally successful, we never really questioned it.

Now that paint equipment is nearing the end of its useful life and needs replacement. This time we're raising the strategic issue: Is this a business we want to be in? If so, how should we best serve those markets? Once we answer these questions against the backdrop of our strategy, we can make the operational decisions regarding the type and extent of investment to be made, if any.

What impedes strategic thinking?

JIM FELKER: At Varity Corporation, our tractors and spare parts are manufactured in the United Kingdom, France, and Italy and are sold in one hundred sixty countries.

We were organized geographically, and everybody tended to look at a particular tractor model as, say, the Brazilian model, or the U.S. or Swedish model. As we looked at a worldwide strategy, those political boundaries were tough to overcome.

VICTOR RICE: I came in as the CEO of Varity Corporation—in those days we were called Massey-Ferguson, Ltd.—in September of 1978, and by January of 1979 I had changed the entire top management team and was ready to set strategy. That's when we ran up against the internal boundaries.

The nature and direction of our business had to be reexamined, and that was very painful for many in the company. We went through a two- or three-year period where many people were convinced that I had a passionate desire to wipe us out of the farm equipment business. You could almost hear some people saying, "We're Massey-Ferguson. We've been around for one hundred and forty years. The downturn in the farm equipment industry is temporary, and this guy at the top is trying to change our direction. If we just keep our heads down, he'll go away."

People feel comfortable where they are operationally. Strategic change can be very threatening. The challenge is to increase the speed at which people can be brought along.

Taken together, these remarks show that without a clear strategy and the support to make it work, operations wins out. There is great pressure to remain focused on operations: There is no great tradition or heritage for strategic thinking in many organizations; the skill to set and implement strategy is sometimes missing; and there are barriers to strategy, such as an inflexible organizational structure and fear of change. All this makes strategic thinking and action a tough challenge. But it is not insurmountable. The first step requires finding the motivation to begin.

THE MOTIVATION TO BEGIN

Despite the need for vision to guide operations, there has been increasing criticism leveled against strategy by both business observers and those on the firing line. Some have said that strategy is too complex, too mechanistic. Others complain that strategy is a kind of period piece of the 1960s and wonder aloud whether setting strategy is worth the effort. Senior managers who have taken the time to set strategy are frustrated because there is little to show for all the effort except, perhaps, the customary three-ring binder in a desk drawer.

We also have heard middle managers grumble about strategic planning. "Our planning cycle is once again upon us—this too shall pass." Or "The sooner I fill out all these forms, the quicker I can get back to real work." Or "Here we go again, another new VP of strategic planning, another new approach with the same old results." The irony in all the criticism is that strategy is on the run at a time when the need for visionary thinking has never been greater.

But the organizations we have worked with see the value of thinking and acting strategically. What prompts them? There are a number of reasons, some of which may parallel your own situation and offer you opportunities to become more strategic in what you do.

THE URGE FOR VISION

Here are the basic reasons that motivate the executives we work with to think and act strategically:

The need to control the organization's destiny

Several years ago, a number of economists believed that American companies, especially conglomerates and large multinationals, were becoming insulated from the ravages of economic cycles. Their size and expanse made these companies more or less invincible. The practical experiences of executives we have worked with do not support this point of view. They know how fragile and vulnerable their organizations are and want to take command of their destinies.

No one knew the need to take command of the future better than Bob Morison, whose organization was being buffeted by an assortment of future shocks and threats prevailing in the Canadian market:

> Consumers Packaging was blocked from investing in new glass plants because of the high capital requirements. In the United States, the glass industry was in a state of excess capacity and price cutting. Competitive materials, such as plastics and new forms of paper packaging, were emerging. New competitors were springing up. Restrictive government legislation was contemplated. Environmentally,

there was a litter problem, which became an energy problem, which converted into a solid-waste problem.

We were also facing internal threats. We had some really good people who were not going to hang around if the company did not grow. All this led us to ask ourselves, "What do we need to be in order to survive and grow?"

Durwood Chalker faced a different situation. The question before his organization was "How do we invest wisely for the future?" Before he could worry about formulating a strategy for the Central and South West Corporation, two fires had to be extinguished. One was cleaning up a nuclear power plant in which the company had invested $275 million. The other was tying together electrical utilities in four states.

With these problems essentially resolved and with an ambitious construction program we had undertaken now completed, I felt that within ten years we would become a cash cow. We had to diversify to capitalize on the projected positive cash flow.

I said, "Let's not sit here and live or die with one business." We could vertically integrate, or we could diversify.

We needed to take a conscious look at holding-company strategy because the electric-utility business was going through a metamorphosis.

If you are aware of changes, a focused direction allows you to do something about them as the situation evolves.

Bill Teague's urge to set and control the destiny of his organization was conditioned by his personal conviction that Abilene Christian University should reach beyond its modest presence in Texas to become a leader in American education.

I wanted to set in motion principles, programs, and performance that would allow the institution to become a nationally recognized university. This could not be accomplished until we had a firm understanding of what we wanted to be and the knowledge that we had the resources to get there.

In my research, I found we had a large number of faculty members who were a good deal better than they thought they were. With that considerable resource strength, I felt that if we went through the strategic process, it would support my aim and be a strengthening experience for the faculty.

The realization that relying on current operational success is no guarantee for the future

The danger with operational thinking done in a strategic vacuum is that it proceeds from where you are now. It assumes the world will stay pretty much as is and that what you are currently doing will continue to pay off. The people we have worked with know this to be an unsafe assumption.

Shigeo Iiyama of the Fuji Photo Film Company spoke about the need for strategic thinking as the end approaches for Japan's high-growth era:

> This means that the total emphasis on "how" [operations] is over. We are entering a new "what" [vision] era. Right now, our company is weak in the "what" area. We feared this weakness, and that is why we feel the need to set strategy.
>
> We have done an excellent job in our core business, photographic film. Our objective is to add another key business in the area of "mechatronics" [a combination of mechanics and electronics]. This new direction represents a consensus of all Fuji Photo people, but it is too broad for the development of action plans. Therefore, we must think much more specifically about our strategy.

Richard Smucker of The J. M. Smucker Company commented on the inadequacy of planning in the competitive food business:

> Our plan basically said, "This is where we are today. Assuming we continue to do what we are doing well today,

this is what we will look like in the future." That's not
strategic. By looking at what we wanted to be, and not just
projecting from the present, we at least had the opportunity to form our own destiny.

Larry Stordahl of the OTC Group said it all in a few words:

One of the dangers of operational planning without a
strategy is that that type of planning is rearview-mirror
driving. It looks backward at what has been done and
assumes things will continue as they have in the past.

The need to get out of current trouble

Organizations are somewhat like nations. They have a history
and a memory. Recent trauma tends to be a powerful teacher.
While none of the organizations we worked with have been
through a Reign of Terror or a Russian Revolution, some have
been through very rough times. A well-thought-out vision,
along with effective operations, is the surest way to relegate
current troubles to the realm of ancient history.

Varity Corporation enjoyed a period of prosperity in the
early 1970s when there was a boom in agricultural equipment.
Then the company ran into severe difficulties. It was at this
point in time that Victor Rice joined Varity. He commented:

Less than a month after my appointment as CEO, I
managed to produce—or at least report—the largest loss
in the history of Canadian business: 257 million U.S.
dollars. We were wiping out equity very quickly.

In January 1979, I said, "We're going to develop a
strategy." Developing a fifteen-year strategy was a bit
absurd. I wasn't sure we were going to survive until
lunchtime. It wasn't some huge flash of inspiration.
Rather, it was saying, "This company has serious problems.
Things can be done to correct those problems. Before we
do, we'd better take time to turn over every stone in the
company and decide what it is we're going to be. Then we
can take corrective action in light of that vision."

In our experience, achieving strategic clarity is the first step toward extricating an organization from operational difficulty. But it sometimes may be necessary to clear the decks of operational problems before proceeding with directional issues. Karen Horn of The Federal Reserve Bank of Cleveland talked about the need to resolve current difficulties *before* focusing on setting future strategy:

> Federal reserve banks are graded against each other by an accounting system that measures all banks against the same kinds of activities.
>
> When I took over this institution, we were ranked in the bottom half. This situation had to be turned around. There was a period of many months of developing new systems and refinements. When this period ended, we were in the top half of the banks in our system. At that point, we could turn our attention to what we were going to do in the future.

The need for a common vision and a sense of teamwork

This situation was a common denominator for just about every organization we have worked with. And it should be for you. Peter Aubusson of the Courtaulds Fabrics Group described the difficulty of an unshared vision:

> Prior to setting strategy, we did not have a common vision. Allan Nightingale [the managing director] was the only one who had vigorously thought through a vision of where he wanted to take things. One or two of the other senior managers had visions, but they were flabby and never were challenged. Getting the top managers together and really doing some deep thinking about the future helped us build a clear picture of where we wanted to go, as well as a better understanding and appreciation of each of our roles in getting there.

The need to win more resources for your part of the business

Organizations tend to be competitive environments, especially when resource allocation decisions are made. One way to get your fair share of the corporate largesse is to be crystal clear about the strategic direction of your unit as you present your plans to the next level up.

The top team of Dow Chemical's polyethylene business knew its future success depended on winning senior management's support for its vision. But how to do this? Polyethylene essentially was viewed by many people in the company as a commodity business, whereas polyethylene management viewed their division as moving more toward a differentiated, specialty business. Ken Mitchell put it this way:

> Our dilemma was "How do we achieve senior management support for our view of the future?" We concluded that the people who went to the board and asked questions seldom got answers they wanted. Those who could go to the board and say "This is where we want to go, this is why, and here's what we need to get there" often got what they requested.
>
> If we were going to keep this business the part of Dow we thought it should be, we knew we had to articulate a strategy and sell it to senior management. And that's exactly what we did.

In Tokyo, Toshiki Yokokawa of the Oki Electronic Devices Group also knew that a poorly defined strategy would not command resources:

> We had a divisional strategy. No one knew what it was but us. The strategy was vague. We wanted to communicate it in order to have the company invest in projects that we knew were critical to our division's future. To do this, we had to clarify the strategy so that others could understand it and give us the resources that were needed.

The need to exploit a major new opportunity or threat

Operations are on target. The organization's general direction is right on course. Then a new and unexpected technological breakthrough or a significant sociopolitical change triggers the need to rethink the strategic direction. Tom Tinmouth of Consumers Packaging faced just such a situation:

> The free-trade agreement between Canada and the United States will cause us to reexamine our strategy. We'll be playing in an entirely different ball game. Success will not be a function of how effective we have been in the past or are now.
>
> This agreement will add only 10 percent to the potential for American companies, but theoretically it will add 90 percent to the total market available to Canadian companies. The difficulty is that all of our plants are geared to servicing our current Canadian market. Our machines are sized for shorter runs with lots of job changes. U.S. glass and plastics packaging plants are completely different from ours. They're geared for longer and larger production runs.
>
> We have this grace period to decide how we're going to modify our operations and change our marketing and distribution concepts to compete in this very different market.

The need to pass the torch, carry the torch

We visited Buzz Kaplan, chairman of the OTC Group, on his last day with the company. It was a family-owned business, founded in 1925 by Kaplan's father. The business was sold in 1985, and for the first time, it would be led by a new team of managers. We asked Kaplan what legacy he left the company.

> I recall the John Deere Company coming to us years ago and saying, "We've got a new line of tractors, and we need maintenance tools to service them." We jumped at the opportunity to provide such tools to Deere's dealerships. Deere's suppliers were asleep at the switch. They weren't responsive.
>
> This desire to cater to the customers' needs was always essential to us. It became part of our heritage. People who

are here today just assumed this to be the case but never understood why or how it got to be that way.

I never communicated to the people currently running the business the reasons for our success until I brought in Dale Johnson as chief executive, and we consciously set strategy. Setting that strategy made us examine our roots, and that made the reasons for our success clear.

So, part of what I leave behind is an understanding of what made us great in the past and a strategy for the future based on that understanding.

Dale Johnson saw this same need when he joined the OTC Group. He knew that while the company had a rich history, it lacked an explicit strategy. Johnson also knew that for the company to make the transition from an entrepreneurial to a more focused enterprise, strategy was needed. Fortunately, Kaplan and Johnson shared this common viewpoint.

When Jack Ludington became chief executive of Dow Corning in 1975, he was hardly a rookie. He had been chief operating officer since 1972.

As the chairman, I knew we had a competent group of people in key slots. However, because of our growth, we were placing a fair number of newer people in senior management positions. It was an ideal time to examine our souls, to test our past strategy and look at some of the issues facing us in the future. I wanted to establish a longer-term strategy for the next five to eight years.

MAKING VISION WORK

Regardless of what prompts you to assess the direction of your organization, once you undertake the strategic process, you also must understand how to translate your vision into action.

Perhaps you are responsible for setting the direction for all or some part of your organization. You and the other members of your team have just finished formulating strategy. The strategy is clear and even shows flashes of insight. You breathe a deep sigh of relief, pleased with a job well done.

Now, let's assume you are a middle manager in this same organization. Perhaps you are a product or market manager, a regional sales manager, or a plant or distribution manager. You may manage a subfunction in personnel, research and development, or management information systems. You may be a significant individual contributor. From the organization's grapevine comes the message that a new strategy is on the way. You wonder how long it will take for the official word to come down from the top. You begin to ask yourself, Where should my function be going? How will my operation tie in? Past experience tells you it may be a long wait for answers. Perhaps your only information will come from studying the moves senior management begins to make. From your vantage point, the strategy job is not "done." It has yet to begin.

Five years ago, this scenario was common. Organizations were a kind of divided self. On the one hand, strategy was said to be the exclusive terrain of the CEO and the small group that surrounded him. On the other hand, those below the top team needed to understand the strategy but were largely ignored. After all, their job was operational. A strategic gulf existed across the organization between those who set the vision and those who had to make it work.

This gulf was brought home to us in 1980, when we commissioned an independent survey of the organizations we worked with. We found that the great time and effort the top team had spent in formulating a strategy did not necessarily translate into action down the line. Since then, however, the strategic interests of executives and managers inside and outside these organizations have shifted and expanded. So have ours. Along with the question "How do we articulate the future vision of our organization?" comes the question "How do we ensure that management's vision of the future drives the operations of the organization?"

When Bill Hendricks of The Federal Reserve Bank of Cleveland finished formulating strategy with other members of the bank's top team, he felt little sense of euphoria or relief. He knew there remained a great challenge ahead:

> Throughout the formulation process, I knew that at some point this phase of the task would come to an end. How, then, were we to deal with all the strategic work we had done? This question was always on my mind. We spent all this time and money and had all this enlightenment. Now we had to make all of it work for us.

One reason managers are somewhat intimidated by the implementation of strategy is that not too much is known about how to convert an organization's vision to reality. Lee Shobe of Dow Chemical pointed out that there is no better test of a manager's mettle than seeing his ability to convert an idea to action:

> The definition of the precise strategy is not as important as having one and implementing it. If you take all the strategic options available to an organization, any average group of managers could narrow them down to a couple. They might be wrong, but I wonder by how much. It is the application of the strategy to the operational side that makes the qualitative difference in performance—and it takes considerable effort and subtlety to do so.

THE STRATEGY/OPERATIONS CONTINUUM

When we began our work in strategy with organizations in the early 1970s, we insisted that strategy and operations be clearly separated. That insistence stemmed largely from the widespread confusion between strategy and operational long-range planning. Whenever long-range planning was used as an instrument for setting strategy, it inevitably diminished or killed the organizations' strategic thinking.*

This separation of strategy and operations was viable as long as our focus was on clarifying vision or strategic direction. However, as we began working more closely with organizations

* The reasons for this are set forth in *Top Management Strategy*, Benjamin B. Tregoe and John W. Zimmerman (New York: Simon and Schuster, 1980), pp. 23–27.

to implement strategy, we found that this separation was really artificial. Going from formulating vision to implementing it was more like proceeding gradually along a continuum than crossing over a bridge or a series of bridges to unrelated territory.

To the left of the continuum is the intuitive, future vision of the organization, which is in the heads and hearts of the top management team. To the right is operations: specific product, market, and capability plans and budgets that translate vision into action. Along the continuum, strategic thinking shades almost imperceptibly into operations. Both blend together in action. Bob Lentz, senior vice-president of Huntington Bancshares, described the process:

> Strategy implementation is a mind-set which enables you to do your day-to-day job in light of your company's strategy. At some point, the strategic planning and the operational planning at Huntington Bancshares will blend together, and you will not be able to determine where one begins and the other ends. We have time lines to evaluate that. But from the manager's perspective, it's imperative that strategic planning be embraced and be part of the day-to-day activities.

We define vision or strategy as *the framework which guides those choices that determine the nature and direction of an organization.* It is *what* an organization wants to be. We define operations as the day-to-day planning and decision making which guide the processes of development, manufacture, distribution, marketing, sales, and servicing of an organization's products or services along the way to its customers. It is *how* an organization is run. The continuum begins with getting vision articulated and ends when that vision is an integral part of day-to-day operations. To accomplish this, three broad points along the continuum must be addressed:

1. *Articulating your vision and formulating a focused, strategic direction.* This requires the integration of these choices: the direction or thrust for future business development; future product and market scope, emphasis, and mix;

capability or resource requirements; growth and return expectations.

2. *Linking that vision to operational plans and budgets.* This includes developing specific product, market, and capability projects that respond to the integrated or focused strategic choices, and then building those projects into operating plans and budgets.

3. *Ensuring that the strategy is effectively implemented, maintained, and revised.* This includes developing indicators of success, tracking key assumptions, resolving critical issues, and planning for ongoing review and update.

Accomplishing all of the tasks within each of these three broad points requires extensive participation down through the organization.

A CONCLUDING WORD

The executives, managers, and key employees of the organizations we have worked with see the need to clarify and sharpen the future vision of their organizations. They are aware of the power of operations to overwhelm strategy and are committed to preventing this from happening. They know that strategy should guide operations instead of current operational thinking determining direction. They are committed to translating future vision into specific action plans on the job.

Wherever vision is discussed, whether in the manager's office, from the church pulpit, or on the political platform, there is a temptation to wax poetic. This is not surprising. So much of who we are can be defined by where we are going. It is a subject that lends itself to a little philosophical reflection and a good deal of rhetoric. Yet there is a tough, pragmatic side to vision which binds together everyone from the CEO to the worker on the assembly line. Richard Smucker of The J. M. Smucker Company told us:

You either control your own destiny or let outside forces control it for you. The importance of vision is that it gives you that control. The person on the assembly line's future livelihood depends on the direction the company takes. If the company does not have vision, and the marketplace or some other outside force determines where the company is going, there may not be a company left. The person on the line, along with everyone else, will be out of a livelihood.

For the top team, having a vision means having greater control over the future; for those down the line, it means that in terms of job security, the odds favor tomorrow.

CHAPTER II
Defining Your Vision

THE NEED FOR COMMON VISION

We have never met a senior manager whose mind was a blank slate when it came to strategic thinking. But his sense of strategic direction may not always be clearly articulated. It may be rooted in his unconscious and vaguely come to the surface only when key product, market, or acquisition decisions are made. No matter how much of it is hidden, however, some notion about where the organization should be headed is always "there."

This is both good and bad news. Since strategic thinking does not begin in a vacuum, the good news is that management's "gut feel" is a gold mine for setting strategy. It is the starting point for all strategic deliberation. But without a clearly articulated strategy, what is "there" in the heads of key people may represent different, even conflicting visions of the future. Differences in experience, judgment, values, functional responsibility, and the like provide different launching pads to the future and different interpretations of what should be. These different interpretations must be made visible and must be resolved for the organization to move forward successfully.

At the R. P. Foundation Fighting Blindness, time was running out for two daughters of one of its founding members. They were victims of retinitis pigmentosa, a degenerative disease of the retina. Soon, the young girls would be blind.

The foundation had been established to fund basic scientific and clinical research to discover the cause and a cure for the disease. Yet, what could be done for these young girls and thousands like them who needed immediate attention because they would have little probability of regaining their sight once it was lost? Gordon Gund, the foundation's chairman, knew that resolving this major concern required a common strategic point of view among board members:

> The board was operating under different assumptions about what each of us at the foundation felt was important. Should the foundation divert a portion of its precious research money to provide human services for victims of the disease, or should it refer them elsewhere? There was great confusion among us that wasn't getting addressed. Setting strategy brought the differences out. Some wanted to keep the foundation focused on scientific research. Others had a more expansive view and wanted the foundation to provide substantial social and psychological assistance to affected persons and their families. The directional dispute finally was resolved in favor of a renewed commitment to the original research orientation. This formed the basis upon which a future strategy could be set and agreed upon.

Consumers Packaging is far different from the R. P. Foundation, yet it faced a similar difficulty. Executives from different parts of the business met to set strategy for the corporation and found that in spite of working closely with one another for years, there were conflicting visions among them. Bob Morison explained:

> We spent three days trying to set Consumers Packaging's strategy. Around the table sat our chief operating officer, the executive vice-president of corporate marketing and development, the vice-president of administration, and me. I'll never forget what happened. We sat there hour after hour in an intense debate about the company. We simply could not agree on what Consumers Packaging was

and is, never mind what it should be in the future. Some argued that we were *the* low-cost producer of glass packaging and should stay that way. Others argued that we should continue to broaden our packaging well beyond glass.

Here was a group of executives who had been with Consumers for a total of ninety-one years—four people who, I thought, really knew the company. We didn't have a common language or any way to proceed.

But what are the dimensions of the "common language" and "way to proceed" that Bob Morison mentions? They must encompass the essence of any organization's strategic direction—the products or services it offers and the markets and customers it serves.

DEFINING THE DIMENSIONS OF VISION: FIVE KEY QUESTIONS

We have found that there are five key questions that must be asked and answered for an organization's vision to be clear and focused. These questions are:

1. What is the thrust or focus for future business development?

2. What is the scope of products and markets that will—and will not—be considered?

3. What is the future emphasis or priority and mix for products and markets that fall within that scope?

4. What key capabilities are required to make strategic vision happen?

5. What does this vision imply for growth and return expectations?

These questions require discussion and illustration.

1. What is the thrust or focus for future business development?

There is a wide range of opportunities for future business development facing just about every organization: deeper penetration of current markets with existing or improved products; expanding to new markets with current or improved products; developing or acquiring new products for current markets; developing new products for new markets.

No organization can pursue all future business development options simultaneously. If it does, scarce resources become dissipated, as do the creativity and energy of those involved. Focus is lost, and with it goes the discipline to achieve the vision.

Showa Denko K.K. now has the technological capability to manufacture a highly innovative plastics container which can be burned like paper but without pollution. And it imparts no taste to the contents. Yoshihiro Hirose cited the importance of strategic focus in determining the future of this exciting technological capability:

> We needed strategic thinking to help us decide how to promote this innovation. And, once generated, this idea must be kept focused within our overall direction.
>
> We must decide whether or not to develop this technology into products for our customers or to sell or license this capability to others.

The J. M. Smucker Company focuses its strategy on exploiting the competitive advantage of current products. Bill Boyle illustrated how that strategy affects the thrust for future business development:

> It's a stick-to-one's-knitting approach, not being diverted by tangents. We are quite content with current product categories, or adaptations of them. We are not agonizing over the fact that we are not in a whole range of other product categories. We're convinced that there is ample opportunity for growth and profitability within our

present product categories. Our thrust will be for new markets.

2. What is the scope of products and markets that will— and will not—be considered?

Thrust for future business development provides a broad definition for future product and market direction. The organization will feature either new customers for current products or new products for current customers, but not both. Within that thrust, how should an organization limit the scope of products to be offered and customers to be served?

By "scope" we mean a set of common characteristics or standards which describe the extent or boundary within which future product and market choices can be made. When these characteristics are clearly defined, managers can separate those product and market choices which fall outside the organization's strategy from those that fall within it.

The Courtaulds Fabrics Group has a precise description of the future scope of products and markets. Geoff Woods of the Fabric Weaving business explained what this description means and its practical consequences:

> We agreed on the ideal product and market characteristics that all future products and markets must meet, and use this thinking to test our existing products and markets. It provided us with a tight framework for decision making.
>
> There were some businesses we were happy to unload. Five to ten percent of our total sales were with the Soviet Union. Even though our strategy emphasized the desirability of export, we nevertheless decided that we were not going to export to the Soviet Union. That violated a strategic characteristic around our market scope: We couldn't control, or have much influence over, the purchasing decisions. We didn't feel we had a firm basis for an ongoing business that we wanted to put effort into. So we opted out of that business.

Bill Teague and his top team at Abilene Christian University decided to phase out one of the university's campuses. This tough and emotional decision could be made only after they had defined the university's product and market scope.

> The focus our strategy produced caused us to get away completely from a branch campus in Dallas to which we had a considerable attachment. We got into this affiliation for a good reason: religious fellowship research. It was a two-year school, away from our campus, and our faculty had little input and no control.
>
> The graduates wore our name, but were not our quality. Yet it was only when we set strategy and concluded that this campus did not meet some of the characteristics of our product and market scope that we set in motion a series of events that led to the independence of this branch campus.

3. What is the future emphasis or priority and mix for products and markets that fall within that scope?

With a clearly defined product and market scope, you have cordoned off the limits of your organization's future product and market efforts. But how much strategic time and attention should be paid to the various products and markets that fit within the scope? These products and markets include both current offerings and those new opportunities on the drawing board for the future. Priorities must be set so resources can be focused on implementing the organization's vision. Frequently, these strategic priorities suggest significant future changes from the current product and market emphasis.

Geoff Woods of Courtaulds commented:

> After reviewing our current product and market emphasis against our future strategy, we decided we were weak in certain areas. We wanted to get more differentiation and value added. For example, we deemphasized our undifferentiated greige, or plain woven fabric, sales business and put all our efforts into the more differentiated dyed fabric business. We used to have something like 70 to 30 percent dyed to greige sales. Now we're about 80 to 20 percent.

Bill Boyle of The J. M. Smucker Company described how future strategic product and market emphasis put management time and effort where they needed to be:

> Our strategy gave us a sense of proportion for our market and product categories. Prior to setting a conscious strategy, we sometimes neglected the principal categories that were the primary contributors to our strategic direction. We were seduced by some smaller new product effort or market center that was exciting but not at the heart of the strategy. We spent a lot of time on some products, such as frozen desserts, which just had no genuine strategic potential.
>
> So, in strategic planning, anything we can do to eliminate clutter in product categories or to eliminate markets that are futile is constructive.

4. What key capabilities are required to make strategic vision happen?

Every organization has capabilities, such as production, distribution, marketing, and sales, which are devoted to the operations of the business. The shape of the organization's vision in terms of its thrust for business development, product and market scope, and emphasis may well require human and physical resources that are new or different from those required by current operations. This is not the typical operational planning exercise for manpower, systems, or facilities. It means determining the strategic resource requirements to implement the strategy, and developing or acquiring them where there is no immediate operational pressure to do so.

But how do you match human-resource planning with strategic capability requirements? Merle Borchelt illustrated how the Central and South West Corporation approached this question:

> I don't see how we can set the human-resource requirements until we know what the strategic requirements are going to be. Once we know these requirements, we can fit

the two together and then go about defining jobs, work packages, and training programs. This is going to require thoughtful analytical work by our human-resources people. One of the reasons we've decided not to develop our strategy further is to allow me to assess how we can tie our strategy more closely to our human-resource planning.

The strategy of The Federal Reserve Bank of Cleveland centers on taking its current products to new customer groups. Since this represented a change from its previous strategy, the bank required significant modifications in its information systems capability. Bob Ware commented:

> To support this strategy, our services management department has done a lot in the last two years to really develop and improve the management information systems. At any given point in time, that department can now tell us how many of our customers are using a certain check product, what their company size is, and where they are located. The people in that department have worked hard to develop a good customer information system for each type of product to support our strategy.

Diversification strategies often require significant new capabilities. Durwood Chalker commented on the need for a new function, given Central and South West's new corporate direction:

> If we are going to diversify as our strategy suggests, then we really have to build a strong marketing function to meet our strategic expectations. We do not have the marketing expertise in our entire system. We must go out and get someone with an experienced background who understands every aspect of marketing, from planning to market research to marketing policy. That's one of the major conclusions to come out of our strategic work.

5. What does this vision imply for growth and return expectations?

The last requirement is to assess the impact of your strategic direction on future growth and return expectations. Organizations that stand still may not survive. Depending on the degree of strategic change in products, markets, and capabilities, historical patterns of growth and return can be disrupted. Heavier initial investments in some areas may be required for longer-term accomplishment. Projected growth or return patterns may need to be changed.

Given its size and diversification strategy, the Central and South West Corporation needs significant incremental gains in diversification results to match its historical performance. Durwood Chalker explained:

> Our net profit is about $350 million a year. If we are going to make a strategic move that consumes management time and attention, we need to do something that can produce $20 million to $25 million a year in additional net earnings. Otherwise, we shouldn't bother.
>
> If this were a smaller business, a million dollars of additional net earnings would be great. I would become a partner in that business in a second. To be motivating to our company, we need something comparatively much larger. Given the strategy, I wanted to have 15 to 20 percent of our net profit coming from unregulated business by 1990—and that should come in relatively big chunks.

The connection between strategy and rate of growth may not always be easy to detect, as Bob Springmier of Dow Corning found:

> I think it's difficult to tie strategy to the growth rate. In the early years of our company, growth was high, but it has been slowly declining as our business has been maturing. If we hadn't maintained and kept our technology on the leading edge, my guess is that we would not have maintained our growth rate as well as we have. I can't prove that, but I believe it. I believe it wholeheartedly.

Answering these five key strategic questions without the hard work of arriving at specifics defeats vision. Even if we assume that an organization is blessed with an abundance of resources, there must be a strategic focus to guide product, market, and capability choices. But such abundance is not typical. For example, most organizations do not have a surplus of talent that is really adept at *new* product, market, or business development or acquisition and obtaining the capabilities to support them.

Given these human- and physical-resource constraints, organizations cannot be all things to all people. Those in command must take a strategic stand. That stand centers around answering the five questions we have outlined. The answers will provide a sound basis for allocating scarce resources so that the future comes about as envisioned.

THE DRIVING FORCE*: THE GOVERNING PRINCIPLE OF STRATEGIC VISION

Coming to terms with the five strategic questions requires a concept, governing principle, or mind-set which provides focus in making the choices these questions suggest.

Bill Teague of Abilene Christian University related a parable which underscores this point:

> When we were setting strategy, I was reminded of the first lesson I learned on the farm. At that point, most farmers plowed behind a team, but it doesn't matter if it's a tractor. If you don't fix your eyes on a distant point and steer toward it, the rows in the field become very winding. Then the mechanical cultivators can't do their work. That's self-defeating. So you set your eye on a mark, and everything that follows will come out pretty straight. In the same way, you really need a strategy so that when someone wants to turn you aside, you can keep your organization right on target.

From the strategic perspective, what keeps your thrust for future product, market, or business development on the mark? What causes you to accept or reject new product or market

* For an earlier discussion of the Driving Force Concept, see *Top Management Strategy, op. cit.,* pp. 39–78.

opportunities? How do you assign relative future emphasis to current products and markets and to new future opportunities? How do you assess and put in place physical and human resources to support your product and market vision? What is the strategic impact on longer-term growth and return projections?

Finding that major concept or mind-set that integrates the answers to these questions is not easy. Three basic difficulties get in the way. First, the strategic concept does *not* include the "standard" operational reasons for making major product, market, and capability decisions—for example, resource replacement, product cost reduction, advertising and promotion approaches, short-term profitability, and the like. Second, managers often are not conscious of what vision of the future prompted a particular strategic product or market decision. Third, that vision may be biased by the experience, knowledge, and functional background of the individual making the strategic choice or by those who provide advice.

In working with many organizations, we have isolated and developed a concept that managers have found helpful for determining and integrating their strategic choices as posed by the five questions. This concept binds the answers to these strategic questions into a consistent framework. We call this strategic concept the Driving Force.

The Driving Force is the central hook for strategic vision. It is your organization's most fundamental building block upon which to develop consistent, coherent answers to the five strategic questions. The Driving Force is the primary determiner of your organization's future strategic vision.

The Driving Force, or mind-set for vision, is determined by *one* of eight key variables that we have found to be sources for the Driving Force. Three of these are described below:

The Products-Offered Driving Force

One of the variables or sources of the Driving Force evolves from and centers around the organization's current products. Typically, a products-driven organization fills a long-term, enduring need. This organization has carefully described the common characteristics of its products and will develop or acquire new products that fit those characteristics. It continually seeks a broader range of customer groups and geographic areas through which to exploit its products. Providing products to these new customer groups may, over time, require product modifications that will extend common product characteristics. The competitive advantage is the uniqueness or differentiation this organization possesses in one or more product character- istics, and it will seek customers who can perceive this differ- entiation and are prepared to pay for it. Product development, marketing, and market research strive to keep the products on the leading edge so that they continue to satisfy the customers' needs better than competitive offerings. Typically, this organi- zation tends to have a relatively narrow product range. We characterize such an organization as having a Products-Offered Driving Force.

Do not assume that an organization with a Products-Offered Driving Force lacks strong marketing. Some of the strongest marketing-oriented companies are Products Offered driven. Also, do not assume that a Products-Offered organization never develops or acquires anything new. Such an organization will extend or modify its current products to fill out a product line. It will develop new products that fit within its common product characteristics. It may develop an alternative form of product to meet the same need as its current product. An organization can do all these things and yet remain Products Offered driven.

Among those we have worked with, such organizations as Courtaulds Fabrics Group, the worldwide plastics businesses of The Dow Chemical Company,* Huntington Bancshares, Inc., and The J. M. Smucker Company are guided by a Products-Offered Driving Force. We will be looking closely at the Products-Offered Driving Force of the worldwide plastics busi- nesses of The Dow Chemical Company.

---

* At The Dow Chemical Company, we also have worked with Merrell Dow Pharmaceuticals, Inc., consumer products, and several key functions. We are also working with the Chemicals and Performance Products Group. The latter has a Technology Driving Force.

The Markets-Served Driving Force

A second source for the Driving Force centers on the markets an organization serves. An organization with this direction has strong and well-defined relationships with its customer groups. This organization is driven by the recognition that its highest exploitable competitive edge is the strength of its relationship with the markets or customer groups it serves. Such an organization is constantly searching for new needs to fill within the base of this customer strength.

These needs lead to new products with different characteristics. Product development, marketing, and market research focus their effort on helping customers determine their emerging needs and then satisfying those needs with new and innovative products. New customer groups will tend to have characteristics similar to those of customer groups currently being served. This organization constantly works to shorten the commercialization process from initial need recognition through to the finished product in order to be first in the market to fill a new need. This organization has a Markets-Served Driving Force.

Abilene Christian University, Consumers Packaging, NISSAY, the OTC Group, and the Washington Mutual Financial Group are organizations we have worked with that have a Markets-Served Driving Force. We will have an opportunity to see the Markets-Served Driving Force in action when we examine the strategy of Consumers Packaging.

The Return/Profit Driving Force

Every organization must produce some return. For most companies in the private sector, this means making a profit. Do not confuse profit as a measure of performance with Return/Profit as a Driving Force. While every business, regardless of Driving Force, must manage its operations with profit uppermost in mind, this does not mean that such an organization uses return/profit considerations as the primary basis for answering the five strategic questions. With a Return/Profit Driving Force, an organization's ability to meet strategically preset return and

profit measures is the primary "hook" determining what businesses this organization will acquire or keep. Other synergies
around products, markets, or capabilities may be nice, but they
are not necessary. If a business falls short of its financially
oriented strategic criteria, it is often sold, deemphasized, or
dismantled. Typically, organizations with a Return/Profit Driving Force will acquire businesses rather than develop new
products or customers. The corporate strategic mind-set of this
type of organization is purely financial.

Each of the businesses within the Return/Profit type of
organization will have its own Driving Force and vision. That
Driving Force will not be Return/Profit, but one of the other
seven variables that, in the judgment of those running the
business, best answers the five strategic questions in order to
meet or exceed the corporate profit targets.

Varity Corporation is guided by a Return/Profit Driving
Force. In the next several pages, we will examine what the
Return/Profit Driving Force means to Varity.

THE POWER OF THE DRIVING FORCE

Our discussion of three of the eight Driving Forces was
intended to provide a quick overview of the concept. The
remaining Driving Forces—Technology, Low-Cost Production
Capability, Operations Capability, Method of Distribution/Sale,
and Natural Resources—are described in Appendix B. Here we
will examine the visions of three companies—The Dow Chemical Company's worldwide plastics businesses, Consumers Packaging, and Varity Corporation—each of which is propelled by
one of the three Driving Forces just discussed. Our aim is to
demonstrate the power of the Driving Force in helping to
answer the five questions that clarify vision.

The table on pages 64–66 presents the visions of the three
companies as their visions address the five strategic questions.
But before turning to the table, read the brief profile of each
company and the commentaries that follow, in which the
references to the table demonstrate how each Driving Force
uniquely shaped the answers to the five strategic questions.

Company Profiles

Products-offered driving force: The Dow Chemical Company's plastics businesses

Historically, Dow Chemical's strategy was to build totally integrated petrochemical complexes around the world and become the most significant low-cost producer of large-volume thermoplastics and basic industrial chemicals. Its historical strategy was clearly Low-Cost Production Capability driven, and that worked well for a long period of time.

With the oil crises and increasing cost competition, Dow Chemical realized that it must review carefully its historical strategy. It saw the need to differentiate and add value to its products and services in the eyes of the customer groups it served and began to move in this direction in the early 1980s. Our work with the consumer products and pharmaceutical businesses confirmed that need. The result was a strategy built on a Products-Offered Driving Force.

This Driving Force was further reinforced in our work in the plastics businesses with specific product areas in polyethylene, polystyrene, and engineering thermoplastics. These product groups already had begun a shift toward differentiation, but the strategy work led to a clearer understanding of the implications of changing the Driving Force from Low-Cost Production Capability to Products Offered.

The work with the three plastics groups led to further work on a global strategy for all of the plastics businesses. This global strategy effort, again, confirmed the Products-Offered direction to guide all of the plastics businesses worldwide.

The Dow Chemical Company is a recognized leader in its commitment to managing the complex relationships between product and market business areas, key functional units, and geographic profit centers. Its matrix structure puts a premium on having this clear and committed strategic direction.

Markets-served driving force: Consumers Packaging, Inc.

When we began working with Consumers Packaging in 1981, it was financially sound and the largest glass-packaging company in Canada. Top management was proud of its approach to long-range planning, but it realized that the company had done little strategic planning.

While the present was full of promise, dark clouds loomed in the near distance. Competition in the glass industry was becoming fierce. Glass packaging remained the standard, but other forms of packaging, such as plastics, which were lighter in weight and less breakable, were threatening its dominance. Consumers Packaging was by no means oblivious to the threat— or opportunity—posed by plastics. It manufactured plastic drink cups, dairy-creamer containers, and closures. But plastics was a poor second cousin to glass.

Strategically, top management's vision tilted toward being less dependent on glass in the future. The top team considered acquiring the capability to provide a plastics alternative to their current glass packaging. In our terminology, this move would fill the same need in a different way and keep Consumers Packaging with the Products-Offered Driving Force it had. Such a move had defensive merit but not much offensive excitement.

Top management considered looking at a pure acquisition strategy to diversify outside of packaging. In our terms, this would be a move toward a Return/Profit Driving Force. This move had plenty of offensive punch but violated the company's "stick-to-your-knitting" philosophy. It was just too far afield and risky.

Next, top management looked at the scope and depth of their relationship with specific customers in the market segments the company served. This provided a focus for their vision: to serve a broader range of packaging needs for current customer groups. This Markets-Served direction would entail greater risk than remaining Products Offered, but it would provide the necessary offense for continued growth with less risk than a Return/Profit Driving Force.

Consumers Packaging has been carefully implementing its corporate Markets-Served vision over the last seven years and will continue to do so, assuming frequent review proves it to be the best strategy for the future.

Return/profit driving force: Varity Corporation

In the late 1970s and early 1980s, the agricultural industry went into a worldwide tailspin. For as long as anyone could remember, agriculture had been a cyclical industry, with a kind of biblical seven-year boom-and-bust cycle. This latest tailspin, however, was particularly severe, and although Massey-Ferguson, as Varity Corporation was then known, was among the biggest and best in the business, it, too, was being squeezed. On October 31, 1978, the end of the company's fiscal year, Massey-Ferguson showed a record loss. When we started our work with the organization in 1984, top management was beginning to realize that history was on permanent holiday and the old cyclical pattern no longer applied. The worldwide agricultural downturn was the new permanent reality.

The top team responded by shoring up the profitable parts of the farm machinery business, phasing out whatever was unprofitable, and then seeking ways to become less dependent on agriculture. All this was a wrenching experience for a company whose culture was built on a long, rich history of success in farm machinery.

But to do nothing would have been to invite disaster. The first step meant that the company would reduce its size and volume to the point where survival was no longer in doubt. As the company became less dependent on agriculture, the top team cast about for the proper focus and found it in a Return/Profit Driving Force. The organization would move very carefully from turning around the farm machinery business to seeking new acquisitions outside of agriculture. It began this turnaround in 1985.

The change in strategic direction led to a number of actions, the most significant of which were disposing of nonprofitable farm machinery businesses; improving the operational effectiveness of remaining farm machinery businesses; seeking new nonagricultural markets or uses for current products, such as tractors; seeking nonagricultural customers for its components, such as engines; and finding new acquisitions outside of agriculture. If all this were not enough, in June 1986 the company changed its name to Varity Corporation to reflect the fresh start it was making. Varity Corporation has turned the corner.

Commentaries

1. *The driving force and the thrust for future business development*

The following matrix serves to illustrate the power of the Driving Force on the direction or thrust for future business development or acquisition.

THRUST FOR FUTURE BUSINESS DEVELOPMENT/ACQUISITION

Products

Current   New

Current Thrust

(Markets Served) →

I   II

(Products Offered)   (Return/ Profit)

III   IV

Markets — Current — New

Quadrant I is where organizations are "now," offering existing products to established markets or customer groups. As the arrows in Quadrant I indicate, in any organization there is a push to expand the perimeter of its operations within that quadrant.

But as an organization thinks more strategically and seeks to grow in an ever-changing technological, sociopolitical, economic, and competitive environment, it may desire—or be forced—to move out of Quadrant I. As it does so, risk becomes greater. The key question becomes: In what direction should we head?

Most organizations can ill afford a shotgun approach. Moving effectively out of Quadrant I takes focus. The Driving Force helps top management fire a rifle. As our matrix illustrates, each Driving Force suggests a focused route out of Quadrant I.

To further illustrate, notice how the three different Driving Forces in the table on page 53 have led each company to pursue different routes from Quadrant I. Notice also how each path helps define the scope of products and markets. Thus, with its Products-Offered Driving Force, the thrust for future business development of the worldwide plastics group of The Dow Chemical Company is to take current products and further penetrate its current customer base. It will then keep widening that base to include new customers with needs similar to those of its current customers. This will undoubtedly lead to a situation where a new customer group requires that a current product be modified or tailored.

But in no way would that modifying or tailoring lead to a product which filled a new or different need. Without a clear statement of strategy, such a diversion can easily happen. When it does, current scarce capabilities are diluted, and new capabilities that are required to support the diversion lead to a loss of strategic focus. Thus, with a Products-Offered Driving Force, the basic thrust of The Dow Chemical Company's plastic businesses is from Quadrant I to Quadrant III.

Consumers Packaging, on the other hand, is driven by a Markets-Served mind-set. It will seek to fill an expanding range of new and emerging needs for its current customer groups, and develop or acquire products accordingly. Consumers Packaging's thrust for future business development will proceed from Quadrant I to Quadrant II.

Varity Corporation is moving toward a Return/Profit Driving Force in the future. Over time, it will move from Quadrant I to

Quadrant IV, regardless of whether that move takes it through Quadrant II or Quadrant III. Return/Profit organizations have no particular product and market constraints or synergy, other than preset profit targets, and therefore tend to be managed as a portfolio of diverse businesses. Since Varity, as a corporation, will be headed for Quadrant IV, each company under its umbrella will have its own Driving Force and thrust for new business development.

The simple four-cell matrix shown on page 53 serves well to illustrate the power of the Driving Force to focus future business development. However, most of the organizations we work with use the following nine-cell matrix to organize and display thrust for future business development, given their Driving Force. This matrix represents the real world much better than the four-cell matrix.

THRUST FOR FUTURE BUSINESS DEVELOPMENT

Products

	Current	Modified	New
Extended Current			
New			

Markets

NOTE ON DEFINITIONS

Products

Current: Products now being produced, sold, and delivered

Modified: Current products with improved features, functions, or benefits

New: Products which fill a new or different need from that of either current or modified products

Markets

Current: Market segments/geographic areas with well-defined characteristics now being served—constantly seeks more new customers that fit these markets

Extended: Minor changes in characteristics of market segments/ geographic areas now being served—seeks different customers that fit within this market extension

New: Major changes in characteristics of market segments/ geographic areas being served now—seeks to define entirely new markets with new and different customers

When the Driving Force is determined, the nine cells are then numbered to show priority for future business development. The greater the change in product characteristics, manufacturing capabilities, or the nature of the need filled, the more the priority shifts from "Current" to "Modified" or to "New" on the products axis. The greater the change in customer characteristics, marketing requirements, or sales and distribution capabilities, the more the priority shifts from "Current" to "Extended" or to "New" on the markets axis.

This focused thrust for future business development sends a clear message down through the organization to all who are involved in research, product improvement, manufacturing, market development, and marketing, sales, and distribution. That message says that the skilled and scarce innovative resources in these functions direct their creativity within the thrust for future business development as suggested by the overall vision. Gordon Gund of the Gund Investment Corporation takes the position that effective creativity comes from this focused and even single-minded purpose:

> Creative thinking, whether in business or any other field, without direction is a form of mental masturbation. You must have a vision of where the company is going to get useful creativity around product and market efforts.
>
> Let me draw a quick parallel. The probability of an architect satisfying a client's need is greatly increased when the architect knows what the objectives are for the facility the client is planning. Without such direction, unbridled

creativity will lead the architect—and the client—all over the map. There will be a tremendous waste of everyone's energy.

The same is true with organizations. When the Driving Force, the thrust for future business development, and all of the elements of vision are clear to everyone, the organization's creativity can be harnessed to achieve strategic goals.

Does this mean that an organization cannot experiment with new business development in quadrants outside the one suggested by its Driving Force? Most of the organizations we have worked with have "exceptions" to their primary thrust for future business development. These exceptions, or experimental activities, may well provide the breakthroughs for the "strategy beyond strategy." But they must be carefully managed as exceptions.

2. *The driving force and product/market scope*

The strategic question about the scope of future products and markets raises two major issues. First, in setting product and market parameters, which boundary—product or market—should be consciously limited and which should be expanded to best exploit the organization's Driving Force or competitive advantage? The thrust for future business development provides the answer.

Second, once you decide which scope or boundary is to be expanded, how extensive do you want that expansion to be? There is a need to define the outer limits of both boundaries, even the one to be expanded.

For example, in the table on pages 64–66, notice that the Products-Offered Driving Force of the worldwide plastics businesses of The Dow Chemical Company tightly constrains their future product scope around product characteristics aimed at meeting a fundamental need better than the competition can. However, their customer scope is more expansive. The customer scope suggests that any industry is open to consideration, as long as customers share that fundamental need and have both the desire and the ability to pay for the differentiation provided by Dow Chemical's products and services.

Contrast this with Consumers Packaging, whose Markets-Served Driving Force strictly limits any new customer groups to ones which are very similar to those with which the company's current relationships are strongest. Consumers Packaging expands the new needs to be filled and thus the product scope. Even though the scope of needs to be filled is broad, it is limited over the strategic time frame to consumer packaging needs.

One of the lessons the organizations we have worked with have taught us over and over is the value of knowing which businesses or product and market opportunities will *not* be pursued, as well as which ones will be considered. The strategic screen of product and market scope gives clear direction regarding what lies outside the boundaries of an organization's vision within a specific strategic time frame. Kurt Fleig, Pharmaceuticals department manager for the Dow Latin American area, believes that with a clear Driving Force, you can readily decide if new opportunities are inside or outside the scope of the strategy:

> If an opportunity is inside the scope, we give it relative emphasis and decide what type of effort is needed. The difficult question is: What do you do when new opportunities are outside the scope? Fundamentally, we have several choices. We can follow the strategy and realize that corporate resources will not be devoted to these situations, especially if there are other places where these resources are needed to support the strategy. Another choice is to abort the strategy and let the opportunity be supported anyway.
>
> I've been very proud of the way our people have followed the strategy in their product and market decisions. We've learned there may be occasions to support an opportunity outside the scope of the strategy, but everyone knows it is an exception and knows why we are doing it. This is the third choice.

Handling new opportunities that are outside the product and market scope is probably less critical than handling current products and markets that fall outside the scope. The Federal

Reserve Bank of Cleveland adopted a Products-Offered Driving Force. This meant that product characteristics, such as the ability to differentiate and cost effectiveness, became powerful screens for determining which current products fit or were outside of the intent of that Driving Force.

As a result, the bank is taking a hard look at all of its traditional services. Bob Ware spoke about two of these:

> One is the coin-wrapping operation. We no longer do the wrapping. We buy wrapped coins from Brinks and sell them to institutions at a slight markup. That's probably one segment that we will phase out in the future. Cash transportation is another service that may be phased out. It's provided in the marketplace very efficiently in most regions we serve, and it may not be necessary for us to provide that service to financial institutions.
>
> The strategy-setting process has given us the tool or framework from which to make these analyses and to say, "This doesn't really fit our Driving Force."

With its Return/Profit Driving Force, Varity Corporation's future product and market scope reflects financial requirements, as illustrated in the table on pages 64–66. Also notice that Varity's scope initially suggests that any acquisition be in an area where the company has some expertise. Peter Barton makes the point that this is a careful way to move toward a Return/Profit Driving Force, and over time, as Varity learns to manage diverse businesses, that expertise requirement will become much less important:

> We searched very hard to find an acquisition that we thought made sense. If we were to go out and acquire a company solely on the basis of generating the highest return, we probably would have looked elsewhere. We went into the automotive components business because at this particular stage in our development, it was about as big a move away from our traditional business as we were comfortable making.

We're executing our Return/Profit Driving Force very cautiously. We're not yet a conglomerate with a track record of making a large number of successful acquisitions. In the early years, every move is tantamount to betting the family farm. We'll relax the constraints with experience.

While the thrust for future business development clearly delineates a product and market direction for future growth, product/market scope provides specific product and market guideposts within that direction. This gives everyone in an organization a clear message about what to consider and what to avoid when it comes to product or market or business development.

3. The driving force and product/market emphasis

The primary criteria for determining future strategic product and market emphasis come directly from the intent of the Driving Force.

In the table on page 65, under Product/Market or Business Emphasis and Mix, Part A, the impact of the Driving Force on the primary criteria for future emphasis is clearly illustrated. For example, with a Products-Offered Driving Force, Dow Chemical's primary criteria center around product strengths. Consumers Packaging, with a Markets-Served Driving Force, centers its future emphasis around criteria related to customer strengths. Varity Corporation's Return/Profit Driving Force centers on primary criteria related to financial results.

Regardless of Driving Force, criteria for future emphasis also include more generic factors such as market growth, ease of entry, profitability requirements, and the like.

In any reasonable long-range planning process, products and markets have always been given emphasis based on some assessment criteria. But too often these criteria tend to be primarily operational and are not directed by a strategic point of view. In contrast, the Driving Force determines the primary criteria to be considered. The resulting future product/market or business emphasis pivots directly around the vision that has been set.

In the table, under Product/Market or Business Emphasis and Mix, Part B, the matrices for these organizations are proprietary and cannot be disclosed. Typically, though, we would show a future-opportunities matrix, with major product and customer groupings and current and future strategic emphases, given the criteria suggested by the Driving Force.

The product/market or future-opportunities matrix embodies the intent of the Driving Force, the thrust for future business development, the future product and market scope, and an evaluation of product/market emphasis based on the criteria from the Driving Force. It is the part of the organization's vision which says, in effect, "Here is a graphic representation of what we will become in terms of the products we will offer and the customers we will serve."

Since the future-opportunities matrix is so central to implementation, we will devote most of the next chapter to this subject and show how it helps an organization make the transition from stating strategy to specifying product, market, and capability projects, as well as drawing up annual plans and budgets to implement those projects.

4. The driving force and key capability requirements

An organization's capability or resource requirements are shaped by its future Driving Force and what that Driving Force says about the thrust for future business development and the product and market scope, emphasis, and mix. These key capability requirements tend to change more significantly when an organization changes its Driving Force.

At NISSAY, the shift from a Products-Offered to a Markets-Served strategy required significant changes in capabilities. Koji Hayashi described how moving to a Markets-Served vision required significant marketing strength:

> Insurance is sold through agents. Therefore, the people in our life insurance division are not strong in marketing and sales. Beyond strengthening these skills, we also must develop marketing specialists in fields such as banking, finance, and real estate. In Japan, we typically do not develop specialists. Rather, we grow generalists. We rotate

assignments to sharpen general management skills. But we must develop specialists if we are going to succeed as a Markets-Served company.

Consumers Packaging and Varity also changed their Driving Force, and this led to a redefinition of key capabilities. At Consumers Packaging, the new Markets-Served Driving Force prompted the establishment of a corporate development function. There was an urgent need to hire or train the type of talent who would work with the field sales force and aggressively identify new needs at the customer level, who would work internally with research and development and production to find the technologies and then the products to fill those needs, and who would then work with the field people and customers to relate the products to their needs.

At Varity, the move toward a Return/Profit Driving Force required the addition of significant new finance and acquisition skills at the corporate level.

With its new Markets-Served Driving Force, the Washington Mutual Financial Group is attempting to serve the broader needs of its customer base. The bank is developing a diverse product line that involves the typical banking services, along with new services such as a special travel program, mutual funds, and an annuity. Kerry Killinger talked about the effect of the Driving Force on the product development function:

> Our Markets-Served strategy significantly changed our product development focus. While our product development function historically has been centrally oriented, the new strategic direction has led us to decentralize a good deal of product development. This also means that our research emphasis is now based on grass-roots feedback from our customers through our financial centers or branches.

As you might imagine from reviewing the section in the table labeled Key Capabilities or Resources Required, making significant changes in strategic capabilities is not easy. One of the key capabilities required by Consumers Packaging's Markets-

Served Driving Force is a totally new information system geared to capturing data by market. Stan Hannaford made the point that his company must capture market data in a way that is compatible with how information should be reported for a Markets-Served strategy. This was a complex requirement:

> Moving from a Products-Offered to a Markets-Served Driving Force involves going to the grass roots of every individual economic activity that occurs thousands of times a day and looking at things in a different perspective. We must begin to look at data customer by customer. Every salesman must log in each purchase invoice, his time, and the allocation of his effort. We're not going to get information on how well we're serving a particular market segment unless we capture it every time a sale is made.
>
> The profit-center approach around glass and plastics has to be retained. Our thinking at the moment is to have a separate information system which systematically captures the information that comes across our desks every day—the salesmen's reports, marketing input, trends from trade journals, etc.

Dow Corning has added a significant customer application focus to its basic silicone-technology Driving Force. This puts a premium on carefully determining the longer-term human-resource requirements to make that strategy work. Kerm Campbell described his approach to this issue:

> The first thing I did when I assumed responsibility for personnel was to say, "Given our corporate strategy, I want to build a model of the corporation in the year 2000." That model would include the kinds of businesses we want to be in. Stepping back from that model, we can then ask, "If that's where we want to be with the major businesses, what kind of people do we need running those businesses in the year 2000?" Having done that, one must back off five years in terms of the kinds of people we have to develop or hire and the training we have to provide them.

STRATEGIES OF THREE ORGANIZATIONS

KEY STRATEGIC QUESTIONS	THE DOW CHEMICAL COMPANY/WORLDWIDE PLASTICS BUSINESSES: Future Driving Force: **Products Offered**	CONSUMERS PACKAGING, INC. Future Driving Force: **Markets Served**	VARITY CORPORATION Future Driving Force: **Return/Profit**
1. Thrust for Future Business Development?	• Optimize sale of current products to existing markets • Develop modified products to better differentiate our offerings in existing markets • Develop new markets with these modified products • Extend the demand for current products to new markets	• Provide alternate forms of packaging for current customer needs filled • Seek new needs that require customers with high technology • Provide a broader range of packaging and systems products to fill new/emerging needs of our current customer groups • Initially focus on food at home, food away from home, and wine and spirits	• Dispose of current nonprofitable farm machinery businesses • Provide necessary support for remaining farm machinery • Seek nonagricultural customers for our current sub-products—engines, components, etc. • Seek new acquisitions that are non-agricultural
2. Future Product/Market or Business Scope?	• Any modified new product must fit within the desired product characteristics • Capable of being differentiated by the customer • Synthetic plastic materials • Cost position at least as good as competition's	• Any new customer group must fit within desired market characteristics • Used by large national companies loyal to their suppliers • Consumer versus industrial packaging aimed at filling consumer packaging needs	• From the first year, any acquisition must equal or exceed our return on average assets • Any acquisition must utilize our tax-loss carry forward where it is located • Initially, beyond meeting financial requirements, any acquisition will have some area where we have experience

3. **Product/Market or Business Emphasis and Mix?**

(A) Criteria to Determine Emphasis?

- Products that give us a significant opportunity for differentiation which has value to the customer
- Products that give us potential for a significant position
- Products that are difficult for competitive entry
- A reasonable expectation of X percent ROS in five years

- Customers who have a wide variety of packaging needs
- Requires a high level of quality and service
- Where we have been a long-term supplier
- More than one major customer
- X annual percent return on net invested capital
- Shift mix from 80/20 glass to plastic to 60/40 over strategic time frame

- For any new acquisition:
  — Cash flow consistently positive
  — Payback must be rapid
  — Stand-alone management
  — High technology, low labor intensive
  — A clear, specific strategy
- For any existing farm machinery business:
  — Pursue most profitable products/markets
  — Eliminate unprofitable products or subproducts
  — Find new market segments for current farm machinery products

(B) Emphasis and Mix

- This is proprietary
- Conclusions from the product/market emphasis work have led to a number of specific projects that have been built into operating plans and budgets

- This is proprietary
- Some general conclusions are:
  — A significant increase in plastic packaging as a total percentage of the business
  — The acquisition/licensing of leading-edge plastic technologies to fill new customer needs
  — Initiation of major worldwide research project to make glass lighter in weight and less breakable

- This is proprietary
- Losing operations have been eliminated, and the first non-agricultural acquisition has been made

KEY STRATEGIC QUESTIONS	THE DOW CHEMICAL COMPANY/WORLDWIDE PLASTICS BUSINESSES: Future Driving Force: **Products Offered**	CONSUMERS PACKAGING, INC. Future Driving Force: **Markets Served**	VARITY CORPORATION Future Driving Force: **Return/Profit**
4. Key Capabilities or Resources Required?	• *Management* — A global plastics business organization to establish and maintain strategic priorities • *Marketing* — High-level marketing with a market segmentation orientation • *Research* — Fundamental polymer science	• *Marketing/Corporate Development* — Focus on needs analysis — Add new product promotion and sale • *Organization* — Need for broadened management capability (specifics were noted) — Need for a new corporate development function • *Information System* — Need for market/customer data to support and parallel our excellent product/profit-center data	• *Financial Capability/Skills* — Investment funding, cash flow, self-funding business, pay down debt • *Fundamental Marketing* — Advise businesses and build Varity as a sound company • *Human Resources* — Address management and employees concerning motivation, loyalty, and positive attitudes
5. Growth/ Return Expectations?	• This is confidential • This strategic focus has resulted in much greater confidence about achieving longer-term growth and return expectations	• This is confidential • This shift to a Markets-Served direction produces a good defensive posture to glass packaging alternatives and an offensive posture on new packaging technologies	• This is confidential • Growth rates and company size have been reduced to position for this Driving Force, and the company has turned around

5. The driving force and growth and return

The Driving Force and its impact on the answers to the first four strategic questions frequently suggest changes in historical growth and return and in the projected patterns contained in the long-range planning process. The specific strategic growth and return expectations of the organizations we have worked with are confidential. But having come to terms with the Driving Force, they know the implications on their growth and return expectations and can deal, first, with sources and allocation of capital and then with stockholders, employees, and the financial community.

When the conclusions from the first four strategic questions finally are translated into long-range operational plans and annual budgets, what were initially rough-cut strategic growth and return expectations become more detailed financial outcomes.

THE DRIVING FORCE: LOOKING AT ALTERNATIVES

Varity changed its corporate Driving Force from Products Offered to Return/Profit. When change in strategic direction is so dramatic, debate intensifies. Victor Rice described how this shift in Driving Force entailed reorienting the thinking of everyone in his company:

> The problem with all strategies is that you've got to bring the people along with you. I remember the intensity of the debate we had when we were setting corporate strategy. If we were to shift from a Products-Offered to, say, a Return/Profit Driving Force, how far afield should we go? The truth of the matter is that if we can make money in condoms and ice cream, we should be in condoms and ice cream. But we first have to take the farm machinery company and convert it into something else. That did not go down easily.

Next, when managers at Varity's tractor division met to set strategy, the result was considerable conflict and debate over

which Driving Force would be best for the future. Some argued
for a Products-Offered approach because they felt Varity did
not have the financial resources to develop new products that
would take it away from its historical product strength. Others
championed a Markets-Served Driving Force. They felt that
the tractor division should pump more and different products
into a shrinking market. For example, they discussed four-
wheel vehicles as a possible new product because farmers tend
to be significant purchasers of such vehicles and Varity has a
solid reputation with farmers.

Eventually, the debate was won. Wilfried Sander described
how:

> Our boss was halfway between both Driving Forces. He let
> the discussion go on for quite a long time and finally sided
> with the majority opinion, the Products-Offered point of
> view. He rarely pulled his chairman's weight during the
> meeting, and then only on one or two occasions late into it
> when he said, "Let's stop the discussion. That's the direc-
> tion we're going to take." But that was after everybody had
> had a fair chance to air their views.

The organizations we work with typically consider a number
of alternative Driving Forces for the future. Even when the
Driving Force remains unchanged, there is always debate and
careful evaluation of alternatives before committing to the one
Driving Force with the best fit and feel for their future. "Best"
means taking advantage of future environmental and competitive opportunities, and internal beliefs and strengths, while
offsetting future environmental threats and likely competitive
moves.

Once a Driving Force is determined and there are answers
to the five strategic questions, organizations possess a vision
that can be used for practical purposes. Yoshihiro Hirose of
Showa Denko K.K. described the power of the Driving Force
in action:

> One very concrete result of changing to a Markets-Served
> Driving Force was a major shift in product and market

emphasis. When this emphasis was defined, it became very useful. For example, we stopped producing commodity cast iron for the broad market, and we focused much more on manufacturing highly innovative steel plates for the automotive industry, a key market segment for us.

A CONCLUDING WORD

Answers to the five strategic questions frame vision. They provide an organization with a clear self-definition and a focus for interpreting and acting on all the threats and opportunities in the external environment. The organizations we work with use the Driving Force as the central "hook" for answering these strategic questions. Perhaps you use a different organizing principle. Whatever the concept, those answers must set boundaries for decision making before you move further along the continuum and make the transition from formulating strategy to making that strategy work.

CHAPTER III

From Strategy to Action Planning

PROLOGUE TO ACTION PLANNING

As with most academic institutions, the future of Abilene Christian University belongs to the effectiveness of its recruitment efforts. Numbers, of course, are important in the recruiting game. Too many empty seats in a classroom will put you out of business and fast. But effective recruitment is also a matter of attracting the right quality and mix of students.

Prior to setting strategy, Abilene's team of recruiters traveled the high school circuit "to cast bread upon the waters," as Bill Teague, the president, told the story. This approach generated lots of activity, but it produced neither the right numbers, quality, nor mix of students.

Then Bill Teague and his senior managers set strategy and in the process set clear boundaries around the university's future products and markets. As C. G. Gray described it:

> Once we determined our Driving Force, we took a good, hard look at our student market and decided to segment that market in much more detail. In our future product and market matrix, we classified our potential student market into major areas of academic interest and gave these areas different relative emphasis, based upon our competitive advantage.

70

Now, with our more detailed product and market breakdown and priorities for relative emphasis, the appropriate faculty modified how they worked with our recruiters. This focused effort increased their credibility with high school counselors, and it gave counselors increased confidence in the quality of our product.

Knowing the prospective interest of students helps us see where they fit in our market segmentation and our strategic priorities. This also helps us determine which faculty members should be involved in the recruitment effort.

If a high-quality student is interested in physics, then the chairman of the physics department is part of the recruiting team. He can be a lot more persuasive and relevant than our professional recruiters. When a prospective student is interested in the percussion aspects of music, then the chairman of the music department and the percussion teacher join the recruiting team.

This new way of appealing to our market is a direct outgrowth of our strategic planning. Perhaps this is why we now are listed in the "Best Buys of Education" published by *The New York Times*.

Bill Teague and his team discovered that the pivotal point in the transition from formulating to implementing vision lies in a clear understanding of the future product and market scope and emphasis. Scope, or knowing what customers you want (and do not want) and what products you will (and will not) offer, and emphasis, or assigning relative priority to those customers and products, give everyone in an organization a specific target at which to aim future plans and actions.

The key to successful implementation of the vision of every organization we have worked with lies in linking the intent and competitive advantage of the Driving Force to future product/market scope and emphasis. This means each product and related customer group must be reviewed for fit and relative future emphasis, given the intent of the Driving Force.

Products and markets can be described in page after page of grinding detail, or they can be presented as a single picture, as one clear frame in the organization's vision. The organizations we have worked with prefer the simple visual and have found that the best way to "massage" and then represent the future scope and emphasis of products and markets is through the development of a product/market matrix.

Using a product/market matrix hardly represents a conceptual breakthrough. Just about every strategy consultant has his own variation on the matrix theme. What is unique in the approach of our organizations is that the matrix stems directly from each organization's vision. It is not a stand-alone device for making judgments about products and markets based on some independent logic or formula. To separate our organizations' unique application of this matrix from the many standard uses, we call this powerful strategic tool the *future-opportunities matrix*. The first step in the development and use of this tool is to answer the question: Who should be involved?

THE FUTURE-OPPORTUNITIES MATRIX: WHO SHOULD BE INVOLVED?

The answer to that question is almost self-evident. The same people who determined the future Driving Force and vision of the organization must carry forward their thinking into implementation. Only they possess the depth of experience on how the vision was developed. The team that sets the strategy must apply all of its insight to strategic product, market, and capability requirements for the future.

Jack Snedeker of Dow Corning supported this point:

> If you want strategy implemented, you've got to have the people who conceived the strategy committed to and involved in its implementation.
>
> For the elastomers and engineering industries which I direct, our senior management team set the strategy. Then the key corporate people reviewed and approved our work. They seeded our operation with enough of the resources and gave us enough control to get strategy implemented.
>
> With strategy formulated, our top team's task has been to stay with it and be sure the rest of our organization

comes along. If all we had was someone at the top, or a staff-type preach about strategy, nothing would have happened. Operations just would have done its own thing.

Bill Campbell of Consumers Packaging saw the essential need for the team that set his company's strategy to develop the future-opportunities matrix:

> If you just developed a matrix without guidance from the meaning and intent of the Driving Force, I don't think the same results would be there. The dynamics of working through the Driving Force and the matrix were important to us.
>
> First, working through our Markets-Served Driving Force helped us to see the opportunities and gave us perspective on product and market priorities in the matrix. We saw them together.
>
> Then, with the matrix on paper, we went away to think about it. When we came back for a follow-up meeting, we realized that we didn't have to look around the world for opportunities. There was a whole raft of them in our strategy.

Given the right involvement, developing and using the future-opportunities matrix require a process. We will take you step by step through that process, from initially determining the best way to group products and markets to support vision on through specific strategic product/market/capability projects and how to measure them.

LINKING VISION TO OPERATIONS: HOW TO PROCEED

The organizations we have worked with convert vision to action by carefully thinking through and answering the following questions:

1. What is the most appropriate way to group, classify, or segment products and markets when developing the future-opportunities matrix?

2. How is relative future product/market emphasis determined?

   • What criteria are needed?

   • Where in the matrix are there changes from current to future strategic emphasis?

   • Where there is a change from current to future emphasis, what type of effort is required—developmental, maintenance, phaseout, etc.?

3. For each major change in future emphasis, how valid are the underlying marketplace and competitive assumptions? (These relate to assumptions such as market size and growth, buying motives, and strengths and weaknesses of the product.)

4. How is a product offered to a particular customer group positioned to meet the requirements of the marketplace and competitive assumptions? (These relate to requirements such as product functions and features, pricing, promotion, and packaging.)

5. What capabilities are needed to meet the positioning requirements? (These might include, market research, product development, production processes, and sales skills.)

6. What are the major project plans needed to achieve the positioning and capability requirements? (These might include end-result objectives, action steps, timing, and accountability.)

7. What results can be expected for each product/market project? (These would involve results such as volume growth in revenue or units, return on investment, and return on sales.)

8. What performance measures must be in place to determine that the action plans resulting from vision are on track?

The first seven questions relate to the dynamics of implementing strategy. The eighth question is at a different level because it relates to monitoring all that has been done. Thus, we reserve discussion of this final question for Chapter 4. Here, let's examine further the first seven questions to see how these can be used to link vision to action.

1. Link: Product and Market Segmentation

How should an organization's products and markets be classified or grouped, given its future vision? This is a critically important question. The most significant outcome of your vision is its impact on products and markets—those you have currently and those you are thinking about developing or acquiring. Different Driving Forces suggest alternative ways of grouping or segmenting products and markets for strategic purposes. The first step in developing a future opportunities matrix is to make sure that the way you view your products and markets is supportive of the vision you have set. *Segmentation* is the thinking process for arriving at that strategic grouping or classification that will support the future vision.

Some Driving Forces allow you to move directly to segmenting products and markets. Other Driving Forces require you to start at a different level. For example, each of the capability Driving Forces—Technology, Low-Cost Production Capability, Operations Capability, Method of Distribution/Sale, and Natural Resources—requires you to separate or subdivide further that capability before proceeding to more specific product and market segmentation. For example, The Dow Chemical and Performance Products Group adopted a Technology Driving Force. Next, they separated that overall Technology Driving Force into more specific sub-chemistries and application processes where they had significant expertise. These areas of technological strength provided guidelines for more detailed product and market segmentation at the business unit level.

Organizations with a Return/Profit Driving Force do not begin the segmentation process at the product and market level either. Rather, they seek the most appropriate way to differentiate or group the businesses they have or plan to acquire or develop.

With either a Products-Offered or a Markets-Served Driving

Force, however, you move directly to segmenting products or product groups and market segments.

The future Driving Force may suggest new ways to segment products and markets regardless of how this has been done in the past. Historically, the tractor division at Varity Corporation segmented its products and markets by geographical regions around the world. Operationally, that made sense. But formulating a clear future strategic direction led to significant changes in that traditional geographical approach to segmentation.

Why was the traditional geographical approach to segmentation no longer effective?

JIM FELKER: With our new Products-Offered strategy, we began to ask questions such as: What really is the difference between a Danish tractor sold in southern Denmark and a German tractor sold in northern Germany? The topography, the land, the rainfall, the temperature, the farming practices—none of these changed because of a line drawn across the map or because a river, or a road, was there. Farmers are farmers. In other words, wheat farmers everywhere have a common language. Dairy farmers have a different language from wheat farmers.

Was the Driving Force key to your new segmentation approach?

JIM FELKER: Sure. Given our Products-Offered strategy worldwide, we felt it was more effective to look for synergies or common activities around worldwide farmer groups than around geographical similarities or differences. Then we could alter our basic equipment to appeal to the different requirements of those farmer groups.

One interesting implication of this segmentation is that it led to new uses for our equipment with new customer groups. When we got into grassland applications, we discovered there were a hell of a lot of small tractors involved. They were used on golf courses and for cutting the grass strips on motorways or by the side of every highway. Then we discovered they were used in schools, universities, city parks, and graveyards. The list kept growing, and suddenly we concluded, "We *can* add to our market segments and reduce our dependence on the farm market!"

For Varity Corporation, this proved to be a major strategic breakthrough.

At Huntington Bancshares, with its Products-Offered Driving Force, a focus on specific product offerings led to segmenting the market in a new way. Two broad categories were identified: consumer and commercial. This broad segmentation was refined further.

What was the bank's thinking on segmentation for the consumer customer group?

CARL ALDERMAN: Within the consumer market, we segment by various stages of an individual's life cycle, such as being a student, being recently married, being married with children, being married with the children grown, being a single parent, etc. These aren't perfect descriptions, but they indicate our approach.

Now we're training our banking personnel to recognize customers who fit into those various life cycles. People in one particular cycle are better prospects for a given bank service than they would be for others.

A simple residential mortgage loan would not be a product that you could sell to a recently married couple. Yet you could sell this to a young couple who have been married four or five years, have become more established, and are ready to move from apartment living into a traditional family home environment.

What about segmentation on the commercial side?

CARL ALDERMAN: There, we are segmenting by size of business as measured by sales volume: the small, middle, and large corporate markets. And we are trying to organize our salespeople and appropriate products around each of those markets.

Small businesses can best be served by commercial

officers who are physically located within our branch offices, as opposed to a centralized location. The middle market can best be served with a centralized staff in the main office. The large corporate group is highly specialized. Its needs and product focus are completely different from those of either of the other two.

The Courtaulds Fabrics Group historically had been guided by a Low-Cost Production Capability Driving Force. This Driving Force led the group to categorize products by warp- and weft-knit production methods and then handle customers accordingly. When the group moved toward a Products-Offered Driving Force, senior executives examined the common characteristics of future products as a source for segmentation. This led them to make "end-use" characteristics the basis for future product segmentation, rather than different production methods. They classified apparel product groups around such categories as lingerie, outerwear, sportswear, and the like. These more differentiated product groups were helpful in determining competitive advantage and targeting specific customers. Whether or not a given product within any of these "end-use" classifications was warp or weft knit now made much less strategic difference than previously.

Segmentation: some lessons learned

We have learned four important lessons about classifying or segmenting products and markets.

First, the way an organization segments its products and markets historically is not necessarily the best guide for implementing future vision. It takes real discipline to separate the future Driving Force and the segmentation it suggests from the way products or customers are currently grouped or organized.

Second, keep the segmentation approach simple. At the corporate or any sub-business level, do not look at more than eight to twelve categories or segments for either products or markets.

Third, be experimental in arriving at strategic product and market segmentation. Try different ways of grouping products and markets, given the Driving Force and thrust for future business development. Take your lead from the managers at

Courtaulds. As they moved toward a Products-Offered Driving Force, they experimented with end-use characteristics of future products, as opposed to their traditional way of segmenting products by production method.

As mentioned earlier, when an organization is guided by a capability Driving Force—Technology, Low-Cost Production Capability, Operations Capability, Method of Distribution/Sale, or Natural Resources—it is necessary to subdivide that capability before proceeding to more specific product and market segmentation. These kinds of factors help with that subdivision:

- Manufacturing equipment, processes, raw materials

- Type or levels of skill or knowledge

- Distribution or sales requirements

- Functions performed by the capability

- Products that can be developed from that capability

- Types of customers that can be served by that capability

- Subprocesses within the overall capability

In an organization with a Return/Profit Driving Force, segmenting products and markets at the corporate level is not appropriate. These organizations will seek effective ways to group their various businesses from a strategic perspective, using factors such as the following:

- Degree of risk

- Varying rates of return

- Industry

- Geography

- Capital requirements

- Size

- Seasonality of business

- Cyclicality of business

Within a Return/Profit-driven organization, each sub-business formulates its own Driving Force, then answers the five strategic questions, and, finally, uses the appropriate product and market segmentation factors to establish a future-opportunities matrix.

As previously mentioned, an organization with either a Products-Offered or a Markets-Served Driving Force proceeds directly at the corporate level to product and market segmentation. Typically, this leads to more specific and detailed segmentation at the business unit level—for example, from product and market groupings at the corporate level to specific products and customers at the business unit level.

The following list includes the most common factors for product and market segmentation.

PRODUCTS:

- Manufacturing/operations methods applied
- Size/shape/form
- Features/benefits provided
- End uses
- Technology required

MARKETS:

- Distribution method
- Marketing/promotion requirements
- Sales approach needed
- End-user requirements
- Size
- Buying patterns
- Geographical location
- Demographics/psychographics

Fourth, the Driving Force determines which axis—product or market—to expand aggressively and which to constrain or expand defensively. If your organization is guided by a Products-Offered Driving Force, the product axis will be constrained to current products, modifications of them, and related new products. In a Products-Offered organization, the market axis will be significantly expanded to include any new customer groups with the same basic need for the products the organization provides. For example, The J. M. Smucker Company would consider only those new products that fit its common product characteristics, while it may well expand its markets outside the United States.

For a Markets-Served organization, the pattern will be reversed. The axis to be expanded will be the product axis. The intent is to offer significantly modified or different products to fill new and different needs for existing customer groups. The primary constraints are on the market axis. For example, the Washington Mutual Financial Group would put real constraints on developing new customer groups but would extensively expand the scope of products it offers for its existing customer base.

Even though one axis will be extended aggressively, are there limits to this expansion? Yes, most probably. But these limits could be carefully expanded, like concentric circles, as it becomes realistic to do so over longer time periods. Thus, with a Technology Driving Force, an organization could initially limit where that technology is located. Dow Corning provides a good example. With a Technology Driving Force, it originally concentrated its technical and its research and development strength at its headquarters in Midland, Michigan. As Dow Corning broadened its Driving Force to include applications of its technology to various customer needs worldwide, it carefully extended locations for its technological expertise to Europe and the Far East. Having acquired an ability to operate in these areas, Dow Corning now can contemplate extending its research activities into other geographical areas, if appropriate.

With a Markets-Served Driving Force, an organization could initially limit the number of new needs to be filled and, thus, new product categories to be offered. Again, those limits could be expanded carefully over time in concentric circles. For example, Consumers Packaging, with a Markets-Served Driving

Force, initially limited new needs to be filled to alternative forms of packaging. It added plastic blow-molding and thermoforming capability to its existing glass container business. Next, it will look for new forms of packaging to fill emerging needs for its current consumer-products-oriented customers. Over time, it may well broaden its scope beyond consumer packaging and seek new needs and thus products for industrial packaging.

2. Link: Future Strategic Product/Market Emphasis

Existing and new products and markets have been identified. But what future strategic emphasis should they be given, and how does this compare with current emphasis? Where the future Driving Force suggests significant changes in the way products and markets should be emphasized, action is required. But how does all this work?

First, each cell, or product/market pair, in the matrix must be reviewed. There are some cells where a product would never be offered to a particular market. There is no "fit." Typically, these are marked "Not Applicable" (N/A) in the matrix.

Second, current strategic emphasis is assigned to existing product/market cells. The only criteria are management time, attention, and allocation of resources. Current emphasis for each cell is either "High," "Medium," "Low," or "Zero."

Third, criteria for future strategic emphasis are developed. What is unique in the approach used by our organizations is that the primary criteria for future emphasis are developed from the future Driving Force and the thrust for business development that it suggests.

Fourth, current or existing product/market cells are evaluated against the criteria. Each cell is given a future strategic emphasis of "High," "Medium," "Low," or "Zero."

Fifth, cells with new and yet-to-be-developed product and market opportunities are evaluated against the criteria. Each cell is given a "High," "Medium," "Low," or "Zero" future strategic emphasis.

Sixth, high priorities for strategic action and the type of effort that is required are identified. In some cells, a comparison between future and current emphasis will lead to an exciting growth opportunity. The action here is a "Developmental" (D) effort. Other cells may suggest the tough work of reducing emphasis in the future. This is a phaseout or "Phasedown" (PD) effort. Where future and current emphases are the same, some cells may require greater time and attention than others. These cells might be significant cash generators, use the lion's share of production capability, or affect a major customer. These cells need a "Maintenance" (M) effort. Some cells that represent new product and market opportunities may appear exciting but need further verification. Here, the action is "Exploratory" (E). Once the type of effort required to address each high-priority area is identified, it should be noted in that cell.

With all this accomplished, the future-opportunities matrix has come alive. It is a complete picture of the organization's strategic product and market future, a road map for action planning.

In order to understand the development of the matrix, you should see one. Because the specific content of our organizations' matrices is confidential, we present a sample matrix based on a composite organization that we call Vertex, Inc.

Vertex, Inc.: A case study

Since the company's founding, Vertex's strategy has been guided by a Products-Offered Driving Force. Vertex fills a basic need for men's and women's toiletries by offering a limited line of products throughout the United States. Each product has a health-care feature, is of the highest quality, and commands a premium price.

Vertex sells its products to dealers who in turn sell to the end user—the consumer. Vertex dealers are primarily drug, department, and specialty outlets and supermarkets. As a typical Products-Offered organization, Vertex intends to extend and broaden its customer scope. This includes adding health and fitness clubs and department stores in Europe to its customer base. Vertex's primary competitive advantage is the differentiation of its products and services in the eyes of its dealers and customers.

Like any top management team, Vertex's senior executives periodically assess the viability of the current strategy. Several major threats to their Products-Offered direction were identified: shorter product life cycles, highest share in declining market segments, and a much narrower product range than competitors. The top team felt it was time for a strategic change.

Vertex decided to embark on a Markets-Served future direction. It will focus on dealers with whom it has a strong franchise or relationship—drug, department, and specialty health-care stores versus supermarkets. This Markets-Served strategy exploits a competitive advantage based on the relationship with Vertex dealers and the ability to develop new products to serve a broader range of needs for these segments.

The criteria Vertex used to assign relative future product and market emphasis were:

- To take advantage of the strength of the relationship between Vertex and a dealer group

- To give priority to dealers who provide personal counseling and advice to their customers

- To support Vertex's customer profile—health-conscious middle- and upper-income adults who perceive and are willing to pay for quality

- To give priority to growing market segments

- To have a positive effect on profitability

A schematic of Vertex's future-opportunities matrix with its Markets-Served future Driving Force is shown in the chart that follows. To keep the illustration simple, we have provided detail for only four cells in the matrix. In reality, the entire matrix would be completed. When all the work is done, the matrix becomes a kind of metaphor for vision, a concrete representation that clearly communicates strategic intent and forms the basis for action planning and decision making.

With this understanding of the future-opportunities matrix, we provide a range of examples from our organizations to show the development and use of the matrix. These examples demonstrate the power of the relationship between Driving Force, criteria for emphasis, and the resulting future product/ market emphasis.

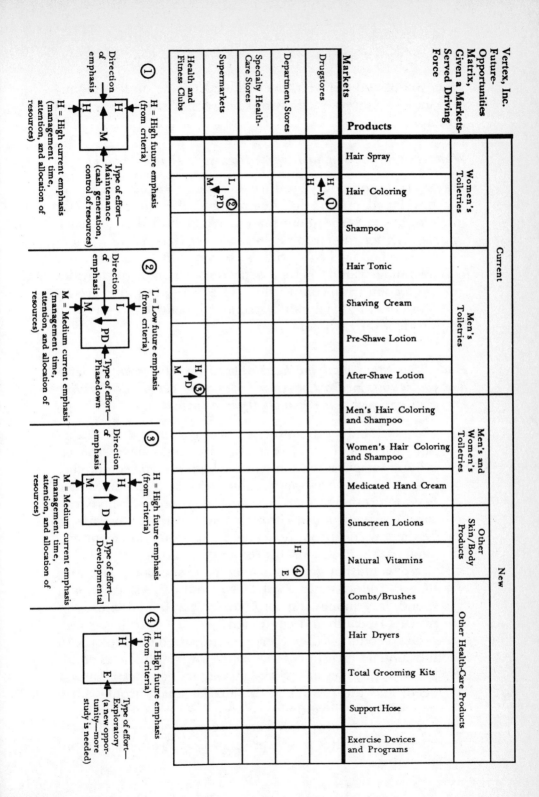

Lee Shobe and Ken Harman of The Dow Chemical Company explored the direct relationship between Driving Force and criteria:

What criteria for emphasis came from your Driving Force?

LEE SHOBE: From our Products-Offered Driving Force, we developed criteria for determining the future strategic emphasis of cells in our matrix. We identified factors such as whether the customer respects our technical contribution, whether he is willing to pay for a performance advantage, and whether a product technology provides protection from competition. These criteria come directly from intent to maintain a strong competitive advantage in product differentiation.

How differently would you have approached the emphasis issue had you maintained a Low-Cost Production Capability Driving Force, as opposed to a Products-Offered thrust?

KEN HARMAN: Had we followed a Low-Cost Production Capability Driving Force, we definitely would have stressed criteria for pursuing some of the high-volume commodity cells in our future-opportunities matrix. We would have been interested in market segments where everybody can produce the product. Here, the only critical criterion is to be the low-cost producer. These cells would be deemphasized with a Products-Offered Driving Force.

We would not go after some of the special applications that a Products-Offered strategy would stress. We would spend less money on product research and more on process research and equipment.

Our Products-Offered criteria suggested that we make a substantial investment in our low-residual, general-purpose product line. Some customers have a specialized need, and the pricing in this market niche would more than offset the investment. With a Products-Offered strategy, we recognize this need, whereas we would have deemphasized this if we were Low-Cost Production Capability driven.

With a Products-Offered strategy, we stress projects where our criteria suggest we can change or modify a product in some way that will cause the customer to perceive differentiation and see greater value added for our products.

At Smucker's, the criteria coming from its Products-Offered strategy not only suggested emphasis on branded products, but also encouraged the company to give a significant new emphasis to industrial products. John Milliken explained how Smucker's got differentiation and value added in their industrial fruit business:

> We have an industrial group that sells the same raw-material fruit that we use in our branded products. This is sold in fifty-five-gallon drums to other companies who then add additional value. We looked at this business and said, "Should we be in it? If so, how should we be in it? What should our strategy be?" We formulated an industrial strategy and asked, "What part of the larger corporate strategy should the industrial group be? If it is just an inventory-leveling function, what are the profit expectations? What size should it be? Organizationally, how should it be managed?"
>
> Taking the cue from our Products-Offered Driving Force, we said that one objective is to try to sell more value-added products instead of just commodity products. So we looked for segments within the industrial market where we could create differentiation and sell more value. That got us into the formulating industrial market. This market has customers with special requirements for the fruit they buy. They are also noncompetitive with our other customers.
>
> For example, a high-quality national bakery wanted to buy fruit filling for several of its bakery products. They told us, "We want the filling to be red raspberry, and it has to be heat stable." We took this request to our labs and conducted the necessary research to make sure we could meet these specialized requirements. This approach helps differentiate us and generate greater profits.

How are the Driving Force and the criteria helpful for determining emphasis?

ZUHEIR SOFIA: The matrix helped us to define what business we really wanted Huntington Bancshares to be in. For example, after we applied the criteria for emphasis, we concluded that we would be in the commercial lending business in the small business market, and in the lower end of the middle market. That rules out spending a lot of money pursuing commercial lending to the Fortune 1,000 companies. For the large corporate market segment, providing fee-based services was the best way for us to utilize our resources. We also concluded that we would be in the consumer market segment. We are going to concentrate on the middle to upscale individual.

In addition, we realized the importance of fee income to our future, but at this point we want to concentrate on select areas of fee income such as investment banking, security trading and sales, mortgage banking, trust, international transactions, and cash management. We are not going to spend effort at this time in setting up an insurance or travel business.

The Driving Force, future-opportunities matrix, and criteria that derived from them were the keys to providing that focus. We recognized that we do not have the resources in terms of people and capital to be in every business.

The Driving Force helped us explain to our aggressive managers, who really want to be in everything new, why we should be more focused. It told them precisely where our bread and butter comes from and how we will make money to survive in a very competitive environment.

Washington Mutual Financial Group, with its Markets-Served Driving Force, provides an excellent example of rigorously applying the criteria to the matrix. In the past, the bank had been allocating resources to products and markets based primarily on operational considerations. This changed significantly with a clear strategy.

In discussing the bank's approach, Kerry Killinger referred to its customers as "Segments 1, 2, 3, 4, and 5," which were distinguished by factors such as income, occupation, education, etc.

Would you describe some of the major criteria the bank developed for setting strategic emphasis?

KERRY KILLINGER: We evaluate how a business effort fits our image, how it uses or doesn't use our current operating and delivery systems, its synergy with current products, whether there is any proprietary niche for the consumer, future potential, etc. We try to go through these criteria for products and markets to decide if we're going to offer a product to a particular market segment, and what the priority will be.

Can you give me an example of how you apply these criteria to the future-opportunities matrix?

KERRY KILLINGER: One of the products in our matrix is referred to as Investor's Guarantee. For the Segment 1 customer, we're not going to offer the Investor's Guarantee product, because there is a need for a higher threshold of investment than is appropriate for that segment. Segments 2 and 3 were given a medium priority. Segments 4 and 5 were given a high priority.

Specifically, how did you proceed with the analysis?

KERRY KILLINGER: Using a scale from ten to one, we assigned a weight to each criterion. Next, we compared product/market cells in the matrix to each criterion. We gave each cell a score from five to zero, depending on how well it satisfied that criterion. We then multiplied the weight of each criterion times the score the cell was given. We then added up the total score for each pair and compared the results.

Any surprises as you completed the analysis?

KERRY KILLINGER: One of the biggest surprises was the focus it gave to our resources. In customer Segments 1 and 2, for example, a typical bank would offer a complete range of products. For us, this didn't make much sense. In the past, we spent great effort taking care of those folks, making sure we had enough tellers to service the customers and the like. We found that our corporate resources devoted to serving those customer segments were strongly over-weighted when compared with what we could potentially get back.

So, with clear emphasis, there was less resource dilution?

KERRY KILLINGER: The process of developing and weighing the criteria and then scoring the performance of product and market cells against them told us how to allocate our resources strategically. We realized, for example, that for Segment 1 customers, we should be spending only about 5 percent of our corporate focus. In Segment 2, we should be spending only about 15 percent. The bulk of our effort should be in Segments 3, 4, and 5.

3. Link: Reality-Testing of Future Product and Market Conclusions

The initial judgments about future product and market emphasis in each cell in the matrix are subjective evaluations against the criteria based on the best information and "feel" at the time. This is not meant to be an exercise in detailed market research or in quantitative analysis. As work on the matrix proceeds and high-priority areas emerge, those initial judgments must be validated carefully in the marketplace. You cannot reality-test everything. Focusing on high-priority areas puts costly reality-testing where it should be.

Aaron Jones of Varity Corporation looked at strategic reality-testing somewhat as if he were a scientist testing his hypothesis in the laboratory:

The decision about which strategy to follow is an intuitive one, at least initially. It represents a kind of intuitive hypothesis about future direction that is based largely on the best opinions available in the company.

But that hypothesis must be tested against what is actually happening in the market today and what is likely to happen tomorrow. For example, in our case, we needed answers to the question: What is the real industry size for various types of farm machinery equipment for our new worldwide market segments, such as wheat versus dairy versus orchard farming?

Aaron Jones's question was a good one. Our organizations have found the following kinds of reality-testing questions to be useful for high priority cells in the matrix:

- Does the need *really* exist?
- What are the alternative ways to fill the need?
- Is the need already being filled adequately?
- Can we fill the need with a competitive advantage?
- Will the customer pay for that advantage?
- Do we really have a unique franchise with this customer group?
- Can we continue to be the low-cost producer?
- Is our technology really leading-edge?
- What alternative technologies could shoot us down?
- Can we make money doing it?

Answering the reality-testing questions begins at the corporate level and is repeated down through the organization. This process is not for organizations with fragile egos at the top or yes-men down below. Reality-testing either confirms the initial strategic judgments about product and market emphasis or requires that the judgments be modified or changed.

The comments of Al Doman of Washington Mutual Financial Group epitomized this spirit of toleration for—and encouragement of—criticism:

We asked the people who were preparing the operating plan to challenge our assumptions about high-emphasis areas. We wanted to know what had changed during the last year and the implications for the priorities in our matrix. I think it's an evolutionary process, and our people are starting to think more critically and in more detail about these things.

At Consumers Packaging, the Markets-Served Driving Force required a careful look at three major customer groups in much greater detail than ever before. Reality-testing of the top team's strategic product and market judgments opened great opportunities for involvement. Reality-testing was done initially at the corporate level by executives talking with their counterparts from customer organizations, and then by personnel down the line who talked with respective customer contacts in marketing, sales, product development, and service and support.

Bob Morison explained how Consumers Packaging validated its strategic direction:

> After we developed our vision, we said, "That's what *we* think. Now, what do our customers think we should be?"
>
> We talked to our major customers at every interface and said, "This is what we've been, and this is what we think we ought to be. How does that fit with the future of your business?" Several said, "You have got to do it, because we're doing the same thing." Others said, "That's a very good idea. We think we should do it too."
>
> Reality-testing is a valuable part of the entire strategic approach, and we did it with every major customer.

Reality-testing is not a casual act. If your vision suggests a significant product or market change, you had better verify your judgment right away. A major mistake at this point could put your strategy—and your organization—on the back burner.

4. Link: Positioning Strategic Choices for Action

As a result of reality testing, whatever assumptions have been made about the marketplace and competition have been verified. If some of those assumptions have not been verified, then a strategic reassessment has been made. Now the positioning requirements for each high-emphasis area must be determined.

Here are the key questions that executives find helpful in gaining insight into their positioning requirements:

- What product features and benefits are required?
- What product improvements and new product developments are required?
- What technological support is required?
- What are the packaging and delivery requirements?
- What are the requirements for after-sale service?
- What are the marketing and promotional requirements?
- What pricing policies must be formulated?
- What are the capability requirements involving people, information, processes, facilities, and equipment?
- What are the timing requirements for product launch?

Jim Felker explained how thinking through some of the positioning questions led to interesting repositioning requirements at Varity's tractor division:

> Before we changed our market segmentation, we had stupid situations such as tobacco farmers down in South Carolina asking why they couldn't have a heavy-duty, oil-bath air filter for their tractors because of the sandy conditions in their area. I went to the dealer and said, "Well, yes, you can have the heavy-duty filter, because we supply it to the Middle East, where there are also sandy conditions." He said, "No, I can't. Look at the catalog for North America. I can only get a dry-element air filter, which is a light-duty air filter, and it's no good down here."
>
> Shifting our segmentation approach from geography to farmers with similar needs worldwide meant offering worldwide product specifications based on the intended use of the equipment. This change led to a far different

positioning of our products with the dealers and their customers. Now we could say, "You, the dealer, choose whether you want oil or dry air. They're both available." This required a complete change of all the computer and provisioning systems.

Several of our organizations have made significant changes in their corporate identity as a result of thinking through the implications of their strategic vision and then reality-testing those implications in the marketplace. When the Washington Mutual Financial Group moved from a Products-Offered to a Markets-Served Driving Force, it changed its name from the Washington Mutual Savings Bank. It also changed the company tag line from "friend of the family" to "friends of the family" to reflect the broader range of services it would be providing.

Bill Longbrake talked about this change in positioning:

> When we changed our Driving Force, we began to position ourselves as a diversified financial institution. We changed our name and our slogan. We then went out and did a significant amount of testing in the market segments we serve. We wanted to know whether or not this new positioning would meet their needs, and if they perceived the Washington Mutual Financial Group as filling that positioning.

Maintaining the product and customer positioning requirements is not a one-time proposition. There can be a kind of dynamic tension set up on the one hand by the positioning requirements of the vision and on the other hand by the push and pull of operational demands. Short-term exigencies in the marketplace can offset an organization's strategic positioning unless the positioning requirements are continually monitored.

Lee Shobe of The Dow Chemical Company knew all about dynamic tension:

> Whenever the marketing management people come in to me with a pricing issue, they know I'm going to say, "What's the strategic positioning?" Frequently there is

tough operational pressure to make a concession and quote a lower price to a high-priority account. But the strategy calls for resisting this approach and stressing differentiation. So I say, "Let's stick to the strategy. If we sit here and have this conversation the same time next year, obviously we're wrong somewhere. Either our assessment of the customers or our emphasis is wrong. For now, let's stick to the game plan because we think it's going to work. If it doesn't, let's change the game plan."

5. Link: Specific Capability Requirements

What kinds of people, systems, processes, equipment, and facilities are needed to fulfill successfully the positioning requirements of vision? As our organizations reviewed capability requirements for one or more high-emphasis areas, they found the following checklist of resource requirements helpful in stimulating their thinking:

- Research and development—skills, processes, and equipment

- Technology/methodology—skills, processes, and equipment

- Production/operations—skills, processes, equipment, and facilities

- Packaging requirements

- Marketing/market intelligence

- Sales—skills, quantity, and quality

- Distribution methods

- Raw-materials management/sourcing

- Information technology/processing

- Finance

- Human resources—management, staff, and professional and support personnel

- Public/government relations

When resource requirements are aggregated for the future-opportunities matrix, they are compared with and help to sharpen the original strategic capability requirements discussed in Chapter 2.

Ken Harman commented on resource requirements in general and, more specifically, for a product/market cell in Dow Chemical's matrix:

> We looked at the resources that we needed to meet our Driving Force and our strategic plan. We requested certain research resources to enable us to develop the products we needed. This request was based on our strategic priorities. So we looked at how our research resources are applied to those priorities.
>
> For example, we looked at our high-gloss resin product for the videocassette market segment. We've participated in this area in the past, but we need more resources to develop the next generation of product. All of us could see that our research efforts are consistent with the product/market emphasis established in our matrix.

6. Link: Project Plans and Action Steps

Project plans are needed so that the positioning requirements for each high-emphasis area are organized and put in place, and so that the capability requirements to support them are developed or acquired.

Following are some of the generic categories to consider when developing project plans. These categories must be sequenced for individual projects and further detailed into the steps, timing, and accountability required to implement each project plan.

- Market research
- Product engineering/modification
- Initial product design and development
- Manufacturing/operations—facilities, equipment, processes, and skills
- Sourcing raw material

- Market development
- Marketing programs
- Sales/service activities
- Distribution system
- Information systems—gathering, interpreting, and monitoring
- Cost-reduction programs
- Productivity-improvement programs
- Administrative practices
- Planning/budgeting activities
- Hiring, placement, training, and development
- Communication and commitment
- Changes in organization structure
- Changes in organization culture
- Functional realignment
- Changes in rewards and incentive systems

How an organization links vision to operations is a function of the structure and culture of that organization. While the process for proceeding is generic, each organization must determine its own way to apply the process among all the levels in the organization. The various hierarchies of strategy and action plans must be dovetailed and integrated.

The following excerpt from the planning manual of Merrell Dow Pharmaceuticals, Latin America, illustrates how one organization links vision to operational plans at various levels:

The process starts at the regional level and addresses how each region will contribute to an overall strategic direction for the Latin America area. The area's strategic direction is stated in broad terms so that maximum flexibility can be allowed for each region to work within its own unique situation. At the same time, however, the area's strategic direction is specific enough to provide a framework for allocating resources from an area-wide perspective. The flow of activities is based on a philosophy of continuous iteration, or "recycling" of conclusions from a beginning articulation of an area-wide strategic direction, next to a detailed strategic direction for each region, next to an action plan to implement this strategic direction in each region, and then to an overall action plan for the area. Regional action plans become the ultimate "reality test" of the area-wide strategic direction. Changes may then be required in the area strategic direction, the regional strategic direction, or specific aspects of the action plans.

7. Link: Results Expectations

Results expectations for any product/market project should be extended over several years. An estimate of revenues can be determined from the marketplace, competitive assumptions, and the positioning requirements. Costs can be estimated from the capability requirements and the action plans. Return should be measured in whatever way an organization measures performance on projects.

The revenue, cost, and return from the specific strategic product, market, and capability projects are aggregated. The results of planned productivity increases and other cost-reduction efforts also must be estimated. When these estimates are added to the ongoing business, it provides an overall estimated strategic return for any given year. That overall return can be evaluated against the normative growth and return performance of the organization. Vision or action plans can be adjusted, if appropriate. This much more detailed buildup of strategic growth and return is then compared with and sharpens the original growth and return expectations we discussed in Chapter 2.

LINKING VISION TO OPERATIONS: A PROCESS SUMMARY

In the knowledge that a picture is worth a thousand words, we present the following schematic, which ties together the process flow outlined in this chapter.

LINKING VISION TO ACTION: A PROCESS OVERVIEW

	FUTURE-OPPORTUNITIES MATRIX							
	STRATEGIC PRODUCT/MARKET EMPHASIS							
SEGMENTATION	CRITERIA FOR FUTURE EMPHASIS	CHANGES IN EMPHASIS	TYPE OF EFFORT REQUIRED	MARKETPLACE AND COMPETITIVE ASSUMPTIONS	PRODUCT POSITIONING	RESOURCE REQUIREMENTS	PROJECT PLANS AND ACTION STEPS	RESULTS EXPECTATIONS	MONITORING AND MANAGEMENT*
1		2		3	4	5	6	7	8
• What is the most appropriate way to group or classify our products and markets, given the Driving Force of our vision? - Product characteristics - Market characteristics - Capability groupings - Type of return	• What criteria does our vision suggest for future product and market emphasis? - Criteria from the Driving Force and thrust for future business development - Generic criteria around markets, manufacturing, profitability, etc.	• What should the future strategic product/market emphasis be? - Application of the criteria to specific product/market cells to determine where the future strategic emphasis differs from current emphasis	• Where there is strategic product/market change in emphasis, what type of effort is required? - Increased emphasis, developmental effort - Lower emphasis, phasedown effort - Same emphasis, maintenance effort	• For each high-priority area of change, how valid are the underlying marketplace and competitive assumptions? - Structure of market - Market size - Market growth - Buying motives - Market position/share - Strengths/weaknesses of products and services - Etc.	• How do we position a high-emphasis product/customer offering to support our assumptions? - Features/benefits - Service requirements - Price - Packaging - Promotion - Distribution - Etc.	• What capabilities are needed to meet the type of future effort and positioning requirements? - R&D - Production - Sales - Distribution - Marketing - Information systems - Customer service - Etc.	• What are the major plans required to achieve the positioning and capability requirements, and to bring each project to a successful conclusion? - Market research - Product design - Manufacturing requirements - Market development - Distribution systems - Sales activities - Etc.	• From the major strategic action plans and the remaining operational business, what overall financial results can we expect? - Revenue - Cost - Capital required - Return on investment (ROI) - Return on sales (ROS) - Etc.	• How do we determine that product/market and capability projects from our vision are on track and that underlying assumptions remain valid? - Performance measures - Tracking key assumptions - Critical-issues resolution - Ongoing review and update

*As mentioned earlier in this chapter, monitoring strategy implementation is the major topic of Chapter 4.

There is no single great divide which marks where vision ends and operations begins. But as we move toward the right of the continuum, much of the analysis and conclusions, of necessity, lean more to operations.

Lee Shobe of Dow Chemical's U.S. Area Plastics Group summarized his approach to integrating strategy and operational planning:

> We evaluate the tactical implications of the strategy. To verify our strategic assumptions about future product and market emphasis, we measure the size of each opportunity, the financial impact, and the degree to which it is competitively satisfied today. We also explore how we could better meet the need. Then, spelling out the positioning requirements closes the loop from a strategic thrust to an operating initiative. When you get through this process, you've got all that is needed to develop a complete action plan.
>
> The annual plans are the summation of all that is needed for the next year. This puts requests for resources into the matrix and allows us to be sure we are putting these incremental resources where the strategic emphasis requires them.
>
> For example, when the new strategic direction tells us to emphasize polyethylene in microwaveable trays, then we must have a resource plan to back it up. If it isn't there, we're obviously kidding ourselves, either in the strategic element of the plan or on the operational side.
>
> The entire approach to strategy, from Driving Force to future-opportunities matrix to reality-testing, is ideal for operational planning. It takes away any mystery about linking strategy to action planning.

Carlos Gonzales of The Dow Chemical Company, Latin America, briefly described how linking strategy to business plans has changed the usual planning process. The remarks we quote come from a speech he gave to key Latin American managers who were presenting operating plans and budgets for their respective regions. The group's work was based on the future-opportunities matrix and the priorities it suggested.

Compared to our first meeting three years ago, this meeting represents a significant change. Before, it was like a beauty contest. People paraded their best look in front of us, but what was the long-term viability of all the good intentions? This time, the recommendations are made more realistically, with our strategy in mind. There is a solid base of assumptions that can be carefully tracked.

Ken Harman of The Dow Chemical Company summarized how the teams in the polystyrene business proceeded from the future-opportunities matrix to action planning:

After the product management teams developed their own more specific matrices with the appropriate emphasis, we asked them to go one more step and develop a detailed operating business plan for the cells they considered most attractive. For each cell, they looked at the volume potential, the expected selling price for their product, how many resources were needed, and capital requirements for plant modifications or for doing things differently. For example, they developed a detailed business plan for taking the very-high-heat general-purpose product into the foam-disposable market.

Support and staff functions are also involved in translating product and market outcomes and key capability requirements into action. They, too, must translate the corporate and business unit strategies and the resulting product and market plans into action. Wilfried Sander of the tractor division of Varity Corporation discussed the implications of the overall strategy on the purchasing function:

We developed the five-year business plan for the purchasing department based on the tractor division and purchasing department strategies. Every year we just update the plan, because it doesn't change that much. It may change in the first year, but the overall track of it doesn't change. Then, once each year, we do the annual budget.

Having been through the company's strategy, the purchasing strategy, and the five-year plan, we develop the annual budget by simply breaking down into twelve months what was in the strategy and five-year plan. Our annual plan is the vehicle for getting our strategy implemented.

For example, we knew that attacking cost was one of the major ways the purchasing area could support the tractor division's Products-Offered strategy. A big step in this direction was to establish a cost-reduction department which would manage the cost of the total tractor. We then developed a five-year plan for the new function, outlining the objectives for the department, how it would function and be staffed, and the specific cost-reduction targets over the time frame. All this was reflected in the annual plan.

A CONCLUDING WORD

Vision has become reality. When an organization defines its Driving Force and answers the five strategic questions, it moves from intuition to conscious direction. During this effort, the future-opportunities matrix is developed. This is vision's tangible bridge to action. Testing strategic conclusions in the marketplace; developing positioning requirements; formulating specific product, market, and capability projects and action plans; and measuring results all flow from the matrix. But there is one final question: How do we determine that our strategic action plans are on track?

CHAPTER IV
Keeping Strategy a Vital Force

VISION FATIGUE IS A COMMON STRATEGIC AFFLICTION. IT CAN SURFACE AT any point from immediately after the formulation of strategy through to action planning. You know your organization is a victim when the committees that were formed to "work out the details" of the strategy meet less frequently and with far less enthusiasm. Or when the planning process becomes, once again, a bottom-up, projective exercise with only a gratuitous reference to the strategy. Or when you listen to the discussions taking place in meeting rooms and in the corridors and find that not much is being said about strategy. Even the doubting Thomases are silent.

Organizations are living entities. They have cultures, formal and informal structures, and control and adjustment mechanisms to ensure continued survival and growth. For vision to remain a vital, ongoing force, it must touch each of these areas of organizational reality.

Chet Marks of The Dow Chemical Company explored what it takes to keep vision vital:

> When your aim is to sustain strategy over the long haul, then strategy must become part of the organization's culture, the job performance of key managers and individuals, and the way the business is organized. You know you're successful when strategy becomes a part of what everyone is doing, when everyone knows what the strategy

is and why it is so, and when everyone commits to achieving it in every action that is taken.

More specifically, to check the vital signs of vision for your organization, ask yourself:

- Is there a common strategic reference point down through the organization?

- Have the implications of vision for the formal and informal organizational structure been addressed?

- Is there consistency between the organization's culture and vision?

- Are monitoring systems to track and measure strategic effectiveness in place?

- Are critical strategic issues continually identified and resolved?

- Have periodic reviews and updates of the vision been provided for?

Let's examine these requirements for strategic vitality in greater detail.

VITAL SIGN: A COMMON STRATEGIC REFERENCE POINT

The probability that vision will be implemented successfully increases when there exists a common reference or vantage point. Tim Smucker called it a "oneness of mind" about both the process or approach for setting and implementing strategy, and how the Driving Force, the five key strategic questions, and action plans actually are defined and developed.

Tom Tinmouth commented about how a common strategic reference point helped Consumers Packaging bring on new people and better manage its profit centers:

We have a strategic process that we understand and can work with. We can assimilate a new senior executive without having to go through a long educational process. We can bring him up to strategic speed quickly.

Also, we can take appropriate parts of the strategy process to utilize in specific situations in our profit centers. We can get organized immediately in that profit center, and then review exactly where we are from the umbrella Markets-Served corporate strategy.

Chet Marks of The Dow Chemical Company developed the point that in any large, complex organization, having a common strategic reference point is the only consistent way to carry vision forward:

> In our organization, the plan for a product department becomes the implementation plan for the corporate strategy. The business plans become the implementation plan for the department strategy. Whether the next level down is a string of vice-presidents or product sales managers, the process is the same. The level of discussion and detail may be different with each level, but the process for getting commitment and for ensuring implementation does not vary in any significant way. Vision remains dynamic and provides the context for what we do.

The central thrust for strategic action planning comes down through the mainstream line functions of an organization, such as manufacturing and sales. But staff groups also provide services and have customers, and must share the same strategic viewpoint and develop action plans accordingly.

In the quality-reliability division of the Oki Electric Industry Company, there were divergent strategic viewpoints about quality and quality control. Mitsuo Yoshida explained:

> There were many functions in the plants, including problem solving, developing quality standards, and monitoring technology, that lacked a common sense of purpose. Before we set strategy, everyone in the division had different ideas about which functions were most important and where we should be headed.

Top divisional managers had their priorities; section managers had other priorities; individual managers had still different priorities. We needed a common strategy to help bring us together. With a commitment to a common Driving Force, each function develops its plans with the overall direction in mind.

A shared strategic viewpoint does not mean that everyone must march to the drumbeat of the corporate politburo. Sharing the same strategic reference point leaves plenty of room for self-expression and creativity.

VITAL SIGN: ALIGNING STRUCTURE
WITH VISION

An organization's structure is a kind of skeletal system which holds together the various parts. It is the form the system assumes. Organizations can be structured functionally, geographically around product/market or production considerations, or in a full or partial matrix. For example, Dow Corning and Dow Chemical have matrix structures. Smucker's is organized by functions or departments, such as production, marketing, research and development, logistics, and administration. Consumers Packaging is organized by manufacturing process by major product. Varity is organized on the basis of separate businesses.

Ever since Alfred Chandler's classic work on the subject of strategy and structure,* the notion that "structure follows strategy" has become a widely accepted management principle. Conceptually, what you want to become should determine how you are organized. Otherwise, how could strategy be successfully implemented, much less remain a vital force over time?

As our organizations have attempted to keep the momentum of strategy going, they have learned several important lessons regarding structure. One of these was finding that there is a connection between Driving Force and structure, with different Driving Forces implying different ways to organize.

* Alfred D. Chandler, Jr., *Strategy and Structure: Chapters in the Economic History of the American Industrial Enterprise* (Cambridge, Massachusetts: M.I.T. Press, 1962).

The Courtaulds Fabrics Group made a conscious attempt to modify its formal structure around profit and loss responsibilities for Products-Offered business units. Peter Aubusson explained how his company's new product-driven strategy led to significant changes in formal structure for the home furnishings and apparel units:

> Prior to our Products-Offered strategy, there were two different mills producing and selling towels under their own labels. Jim Connor, who heads up home furnishings, recognized that with a Products-Offered Driving Force, he should be managing his position in the towel market as one integrated unit. So he put one person in charge of the two companies. While the companies kept their separate brand names, their sales forces were combined, and now salesmen handle the overall towel line.
>
> In the apparel business unit, there was a major restructuring around market segment teams. There are individual teams for menswear, women's outerwear, lingerie, children's wear, and sportswear. In each of these market segments, many products are substitutable for one another. For example, a woman can buy a dress or a shirt or blouse. Or, in lingerie, she can purchase a slip, a camisole, or French knickers. With a Products-Offered strategy, we present the entire range of fabrics that we make for each segment in a much more coordinated way, regardless of the production method.

Dow Corning expanded its Technology Driving Force to include a new emphasis on developing a wide array of silicone-technology applications to fit its customer needs. This led it to seek an expanded range of both product and market opportunities. To accomplish the new strategic emphasis, it decided to create new formal organizational units by major injustry categories. These commercial industry units were added to Dow Corning's overall matrix structure, which included business, geographical, and functional units.

Ed Steinhoff commented on how the change in structure would better extend silicone applications to new products and customers:

Previously, our marketing, sales, and technical service had been entirely product oriented. Our focus was on what we made and then finding customers with the need. We decided that this was not the best way to implement a Technology Driving Force. The addition of commercial units by industry allowed us to organize our marketing and service efforts around customer groups so that new product and marketing opportunities were more readily identified.

We put a single manager in charge of each industry group. This manager has technical, marketing, and sales personnel backing him up and can integrate their activities. Before, technical service was part of R&D, marketing was product oriented, and the sales activity was essentially geographical.

Larry Reed commented further on the implications of Dow Corning's Technology vision for the manufacturing function:

Take our sealants business as one example. Historically, the bulk sealants business grew up around our Elizabethtown plant. Everything there related to sealants, including product development.

As we broadened our Technology Driving Force to include specific applications of the technology, we began to add high-value, differentiated specialty components to the basic bulk sealants business. Those specialty components had a tough time working their way through the bulk-manufacturing mentality at Elizabethtown. Eventually, we had to separate the two businesses, and we now have an entire new facility for the development and servicing of specialty sealants and elastomers.

Dow Corning's new application focus for its Technology Driving Force also affects the matrix organization structure. The company recently made a major acquisition to support its rubber-compounding business. This acquisition is unique in terms of its customer base, the needs it fills, and response time. Dow Corning plans to leave the line structure of that organization intact. It is not a matrix.

As the Washington Mutual Financial Group shifted from a Products-Offered to a Markets-Served Driving Force, significant organizational changes and job redefinitions were required. Bill Longbrake explained the implications for customer relations:

> When we were Products Offered driven, we had a residential-mortage lending function with a technical specialist in charge. This was a functional approach in which we organized around a particular product. But having a senior executive in charge of a product area is inconsistent with the intent of our future strategy. We eliminated the technical specialist's position and put this loan-origination responsibility under the sales manager. He heads up a financial center and formerly would have been branch manager. Now his job is perceived much differently.
>
> In the last six months, we reorganized these financial centers to support our Markets-Served vision. All specialists and generalists are responsible to a single sales manager. Even the registered securities representatives now report to that sales manager rather than to the head of a subsidiary company.
>
> Our aim is to coordinate all the sales activities around a Markets-Served direction and have a team approach in each center. This structure really allows us to focus on the customer relationship in its entirety.

Vision may suggest organizational change—structure does follow strategy. But what happens when the logic of vision comes up against the hard rocks of operational reality? Sometimes, the formal structure can be "tweaked," to use the term of Jack Ludington of Dow Corning. But there are other times when the existing structure cannot be changed to fit the requirements of vision, except over a long period of time. What do you do when structure cannot follow strategy in the short run? To answer this question, it is helpful to know how an organization's structure develops.

Structure may evolve because it fits the past or current strategy. For example, if an organization had been Products Offered driven, the formal structure may have evolved around differences in product offerings or customers served. If an organization had been Low-Cost Production Capability driven in the past, the formal organization probably would be structured around differences in those production capabilities. If Markets Served were the Driving Force, the formal structure would probably evolve around major customer groups.

The current formal organizational structure may have developed for sound operational reasons, regardless of the strategy or vision. For example, the formal profit-center structure may be geographically based for legal, cultural, marketing, or management-control reasons. Plants or manufacturing centers may determine the formal structure because of capital-intensity requirements and the need to tie overall profit-and-loss responsibility to these plants or manufacturing centers. Market segments or customer groups may become the formal structure because of differences in the methods of sale and distribution.

When these operational factors suggested preserving the current formal structure—even though the future vision suggested a change in that structure—then our organizations took an interim action. They established an informal or task-group structure to accomplish the strategic objectives without disrupting the prevailing order.

The case of Consumers Packaging illustrates how an informal task-group structure can accommodate the requirements of both vision and operational reality. When its strategy was guided by a Products-Offered Driving Force, Consumers Packaging's structure was developed to support the glass, plastics, and closures profit centers. This was necessary to put focus on manufacturing in order to maximize the return on capital employed. Each profit center or division had its own research, marketing, sales, and service functions. All computer-based information systems were designed to collect and report revenue, cost, and profitability across major product groupings within each division. Where a customer's need could be filled by either a glass or a plastic container, competition between these two divisions was as fierce as any outside competition could be.

When Consumers Packaging shifted its Driving Force to Markets Served, it began to focus strategically on various customer groups with which it had a strong or unique relationship.

One customer group focused on food products to be consumed at home. Another customer group focused on container packaging for food to be consumed away from home. This included producers of individual packets of jams and jellies, creamers, sugar, etc. There was also a wines and spirits customer group. Given the new vision, it became critical to focus on the emerging packaging needs of each of these customer groups, finding ways to fill the needs, monitoring the ongoing customer response to packaging options, and determining which individual customers merited emphasis in the future.

There was no existing organizational structure in place to accomplish these ends. Senior executives at Consumers Packaging considered changing the formal structure by carefully and gradually shifting profit-center responsibility away from the glass, plastics, and closures divisions and adopting a structure with profit-center responsibility around each of the major market segments. There would be a separate sales force for each major market segment, selling whatever form of packaging was most appropriate to meet customers' needs within that segment. Emerging and new customer packaging needs would flow through this structure to research and development, to product engineering, or to a new acquisition that would meet those needs.

This new structure ultimately was rejected by senior management because of the strong need to manage profit and loss around different production capabilities and capital requirements. In addition, the pressures for volume growth, cost reduction, quality improvements, and productivity gains were best managed through the existing structure.

Rather, cross-functional task teams of middle managers were formed around each of the three customer groups. Participation in this effort was beyond current job responsibilities. Each task team segmented the corporate future-opportunities matrix in greater detail for the customer group it examined. Next, each team took the strategic message to its major customers to assess future packaging needs. Then, after positioning requirements were determined, specific projects were recommended to top management.

Ben Goodman commented on the structure of his task team and what he and his colleagues got from the experience:

The team for wines and spirits began its work in February and wound down in the spring of the following year. Our mission was carefully explained to us before we began. But there was plenty of flexibility about how to proceed. No one dictated to us who the team leader should be, or if there should be one. Interestingly, leadership within the group just evolved naturally. Some people gave 150 percent, others 110 percent, and others 90 percent.

The results we produced were much more than the recommendations made. We learned from one another about what types of questions to ask our customers and how to probe for need. The updates we provided gave us a unique opportunity to exchange ideas with senior management and to further sharpen our perspective.

Going out to interview our customers, working with fellow team members, and interacting with senior management widened my perspective. Even though I have been working for Consumers for more than fourteen years, the work of the task team opened my eyes about the industry we are in.

The three task teams now have been replaced by a formal organization unit called "new business development." Stew Kennedy, vice-president of new business development, described the need for his unit:

Our current operating divisions have neither the time, inclination, nor resources to assess the potential of filling a new customer need through an acquisition or a new technology. They need a group to shepherd the effort through the organization without interrupting day-to-day operations.

In addition, we spend time assessing and exploiting all the possibilities of filling new customer needs with the existing technology we already have acquired through licensing arrangements.

Frank Fabian, market manager for new business development, commented on the importance of properly staffing this function:

Making Stew Kennedy a vice-president for this new function gave the effort a lot of credibility. It also let the rest of
the company know that we were here for a very specific
purpose and, if we needed cooperation from a division,
that would be given priority.

Stew formerly was general manager of one of our
thermoforming operations. He brings considerable plastics experience. I was chosen because of my knowledge of
the packaging market and sales ability. The other member
of the group, Zohir Handy, brings a strong technical
knowledge of the international packaging business. Our
skills are supplemented by a market research analyst.

When an organization establishes a new structure to help
implement vision, there exists the potential for confusion
externally in the marketplace and internally between the operational structure that is in place and the newly formed strategic
entity. This must be monitored carefully.

While it is too soon to be categorical, we feel that a kind of
iron law of symmetry may be operating between strategy and
structure: If a new and different future Driving Force remains
in effect for a relatively long period of time, then the formal
structure, over time, gradually becomes aligned to that strategy.
But to know if the structures of our organizations continue to
evolve will require long-term surveillance.

VITAL SIGN: RELATING CULTURE AND VISION

Much has been written on the subject of organizational
culture—what it is and how to measure, change, and manage it.
Our purpose is not to add to the tonnage of printed material on
the subject. However, since culture plays an important role in
determining and sustaining vision, we should at least briefly
discuss the subject within this context.

For our purpose, culture is the pattern of norms, values,
beliefs, and attitudes that influence individual and group behavior within an organization. These norms, values, and beliefs
originate with the founders of the organization and are further
shaped and honed over time by succeeding senior executives and

other stakeholder groups. These values filter down through the organization and are further refined and modified in the day-to-day priorities and actions of all the managers and employees in the business. They circle back up the organization and reinforce and refine the thinking of senior managers.

One important lesson we have learned about culture is the necessity of explicitly stating the basic beliefs and values of an organization. Some organizations have published their underlying beliefs and values. Often, they are stated as "creeds." But in many organizations, values have not been consciously articulated. They simply are part of "how we run the business."

Our organizations discuss, debate, state, and commit to a set of underlying values as an integral part of setting strategy. Why spend the time doing this? Beliefs about quality, ethics, growth, and people, and commitment to being on the leading edge, being the biggest or the best, and remaining independent or being acquired, influence significantly what Driving Force you select; the strategic product, market, and capability choices you make; and how well your strategy fits with and is accepted by the organization and the marketplace. Tim Smucker explained why getting out the "self-evident truths" is no easy task:

> The most difficult part of setting strategy was putting our basic beliefs down on paper. They are very deeply felt, and we wanted to be sure to dot every "i" and cross every "t". The essence of what we believe was not too difficult to identify, but describing our beliefs in a document was a real challenge.

The J. M. Smucker Company's statement of basic beliefs took the top team a long time to hammer out. These beliefs form the preamble to the company's statement of its vision:

THE J. M. SMUCKER COMPANY BASIC BELIEFS

Quality

Quality is the key word and shall apply to our people, our products, our manufacturing methods, and our marketing efforts. We will market the highest-quality products offered in our respective markets.

- Consistent high quality is required.
- The Company's growth and success have been built on quality.
- Quality comes first; then earnings and sales growth will follow. We will only produce and sell products that enhance the quality of life and well-being.

Ethics

Just as this Company was founded and has developed based on strong ethical values, these same values are ingrained in our management team today. This style of management is the standard by which we conduct our business, as well as ourselves, no less of which is acceptable under any circumstances. Therefore, we will maintain the highest standards of business ethics with customers, suppliers, employees, and communities where we work.

Independence

Because of our strong commitment to stewardship of the Smucker name and heritage, our desire to control our own direction, and our motivation to succeed on our own, we will remain an independent company. We seek to serve as an example of the success of a company which operates by these principles within the free-enterprise system.

Growth

As we are concerned with day-to-day operations, we are also concerned with the potential of our Company. Growing is reaching for that potential whether it be in the development of new products and new markets, the discovery of new manufacturing or management techniques, or the personal growth and development of our people and their ideas.

We are committed to a strong balanced growth that will protect or enhance our consumer franchise within prudent financial parameters. We want to provide a fair return for our stockholders on their investment in us.

People

We will be fair with our employees and expect fair effort in return. We will seek employees who are committed to preserving and enhancing these values and principles through their own actions.

- Highest-quality products and service require the highest-quality people.

- Highest business ethics require the highest personal ethics.

These basic beliefs regarding quality, ethics, independence, growth, and people have served as a strong foundation in our history, and will be the basis for future strategy, plans, and achievement.

Another lesson we have learned about basic beliefs centers on culture change. Once vision is developed and the work on implementation begins, some basic beliefs may have to be modified or even eliminated. New beliefs may have to be added. Some beliefs may stay the same.

Jim Schultz provided an example of the need for a value reorientation at the OTC Group because of its new Markets-Served Driving Force:

We've begun to look at how we can be more responsive to filling new and additional customer needs. This means a sales mentality which actively probes for new needs, not one that focuses on selling current products. It means a more rapid responsiveness in developing and manufacturing products to fit a new need.

Given this, we would expect the culture to change from a Products-Offered mentality, where we're concentrating on similar standards of quality in our production runs. With our Markets-Served mentality, there is a need to develop greater flexibility to meet varying quality standards for differing and new needs.

The best way to ensure such a culture change is to take the kinds of actions along the sales, product development, and manufacturing fronts that will support this required change in culture.

Moving from one Driving Force to another does not necessarily entail a 180-degree cultural revolution. Some beliefs remain as is. For the OTC Group, certain values needed to change, as Jim Schultz noted. Dale Johnson commented on other values that remained the same despite the new strategic direction and change in ownership:

> Going from being a family-owned company to having a new corporate owner and going from a longtime CEO who is a member of the founder's family to an outside CEO are significant emotional events in the life of a company. Having been through this level of stress, we felt then and now that our basic beliefs were an incredibly important mortar which held the bricks together through the change and trauma.
>
> Belief in things such as excellence, the dignity of our employees, high product quality, and the importance of our relationships with customers and vendors has not changed.

A third lesson we have learned about culture is that you cannot legislate commitment to basic beliefs, nor can you bring them to life merely by publishing them as top management's latest manifesto. This is especially true in situations where a discrepancy exists between a new corporate strategy and deep-seated beliefs and attitudes of people throughout the organization.

Aaron Jones commented on the powerful grip of nationalism on culture that became apparent when Varity attempted to implement a worldwide tractor-division strategy:

> To shift the tractor division from a geographical orientation to one which differentiates by end use worldwide was fairly radical. There was a real affection by the French employees for the French company, by the British employees for the U.K. company, and by the Italian employees for the Italian company. An awful lot of people saw their

loyalty and interest connected much more closely to what happened to each of these companies than to the tractor division overall.

Whatever the difficulties, the best way to build basic beliefs into the hearts, minds, and hands of people down through the organization is in the action plans for implementing strategy. Those action plans must be consistent with and supportive of those basic values, or they should not be approved. Jim Connor of Courtaulds talked about action initiatives supporting basic beliefs:

> Making our beliefs visible and putting them at the forefront of our vision have led us to pay greater attention to certain areas. Top management pushed forcefully to introduce basic beliefs into the textile group by supporting them with the kind of specific initiatives that demonstrated how serious we were about our basic beliefs.
>
> We reexamined quality standards and operational efficiencies, and moved closer to the customer in terms of fabric style and design. Now I personally check style development and how fast we can move through to the customer.
>
> Interestingly, in some of our new companies, it has been relatively easy to get the message about values through to everyone and to set up the structure to be more innovative. It's just human nature that where you have an entrenched management, or a large company, it is more difficult to effect change.

John Billing talked about the mind-set toward basic beliefs that is needed to support action planning at Courtaulds:

> One of our basic beliefs states that we must have a level of quality in our products to satisfy every customer. This means we must have the capability to specify what the customer wants. We also must be capable of providing what the customer wants. We also need capabilities around the quality effort to move toward a preventive rather than

an inspection process. Beyond all this, we need a management capability which recognizes this quality belief and measures and monitors the action steps to bring it about.

Zuheir Sofia of Huntington Bancshares commented on translating basic beliefs into action right down to first-line employees:

> When we talk about the level of consistent quality needed to support our Products-Offered Driving Force, we take this belief right to the teller. For the teller, quality converts to customer service. That may mean always having a friendly smile, or getting to know the customers and their needs, or making sure that the customer never is made to feel that he or she is the cause of a problem.

There are human, physical, and information systems in every organization through which strategic product, market, and capability action plans are implemented. These systems provide excellent vehicles for reinforcing basic beliefs. They include:

- Job functions and performance reviews—objectives, standards, and accomplishments

- General systems—management information, human resources, and customer records

- Quality and service standards

- Operational long- and short-range planning and annual budgeting

- Human-resource development and training

- Formal and informal organization structures

- Advertising and promotional literature

- Company publications

Thinking through how beliefs can be reinforced using these systems is critical. It is difficult to change values and beliefs simply by willing them into being. They cannot be changed head-on. It is far more effective to build these beliefs into the management infrastructure of an organization and make them part of the natural order of things.

One final lesson we have learned is that being an agent for change does not necessarily require a Ph.D. in the social sciences. Much can be accomplished by old-fashioned salesmanship. Gerry Kavanagh talked about the effect of the Consumers Packaging name change on his people:

> The change in name was hard to accept for many of our old-timers on the factory floor. Losing the word "glass" from the company name bothered the hell out of them.
>
> A lot of people griped because they didn't know the total picture, and they really didn't care about the new direction. They thought that the glass plant paid their way. I told them that when we all retired, the plastics division would be bringing a lot of money to the bottom line, which would help pay our pensions and sustain our work force.
>
> Glass will still be there, but we need other divisions. We're not losing anything; we're actually gaining something. And people are beginning to respond. We're slowly turning around the culture in the plant.

In our experience, culture as expressed in basic beliefs is an "input" to determining and implementing future vision. But beliefs must also be considered an "output" of having set that direction. As an output, they must be shaped to ensure that they support the implementation of the strategy and help sustain it over time. Ultimately, success in shaping culture to support vision will depend on how well we heed the biblical injunction "By their fruits ye shall know them."

VITAL SIGN: MONITORING VISION'S SUCCESS

Vision is subject to all the inherent uncertainties of what is yet to come. Murphy's Law has a way of derailing even our most carefully conceived plans. Sustaining vision over the long haul requires that monitoring processes and procedures be put in place to tell us, first, whether or not we are on track in implementing the vision we have set. Masaaki Shibamoto of NISSAY described how his company accomplishes this in both formal and informal ways:

> At the end of each fiscal year, each division manager reports his strategic plan to his superior. This includes action plans to implement it that are stated as critical issues. Last year's results in terms of critical issues resolved are also presented. This is done typically through detailed written reports. In addition, there are frequent informal, conversational checks at divisional and unit levels on the effectiveness of strategy implementation.
>
> Senior executives report all of this strategic activity to the chairman and president by informal, one-on-one discussions. Informal means are a critical way that we monitor strategic effectiveness.

Second, monitoring processes must tell us whether or not the underlying assumptions upon which our vision is based remain sound. For example, when the plastics division of Showa Denko developed a new plastic substitute for metal cans, obviously they looked at the positive outcomes of this strategic product/market choice. However, the company also thought about the critical environmental factors that could defeat the strategy. Managers had to monitor their metal can competitors to check probable reactions. Yoshihiro Hirose described what action they took:

> If these competitors reduce price, it could drive our new plastic product from the market because profit margins are lower on plastics. To overcome this competitive threat, we plan to supply technological know-how and raw material to one large metal can producer. We are confident that this will improve sales dramatically for us and keep a potential competitor satisfied.

Executives at The Federal Reserve Bank of Cleveland must continually monitor a critical environmental assumption because of its potentially significant impact on the bank's strategy. Karen Horn commented:

> An environmental constraint has played a significant role in impeding the implementation of the strategy we set at The Federal Reserve Bank of Cleveland. While our strategy was not a radical departure, there were elements which were new and stretched our strategic thinking. As it turns out, we've entered a time of growing constraints, given the Gramm-Rudman initiatve. This may put cost constraints on us which will make it difficult to implement the strategy we developed.

The key to monitoring vision effectively is to develop the right strategic questions. Then, monitoring approaches can be developed to provide answers on an ongoing basis. The process of asking strategic questions and monitoring vision must become just as integral to every management planning and review meeting as are operational matters.

These kinds of questions help you measure strategic effectiveness:

- What environmental assumptions are pivotal to the continuation of the strategy?

- What evidence do we have that the competitive advantage inherent in our future Driving Force continues to be realistic?

- Are we sure that resources are being allocated to achieve our strategic priorities?

- Are the new and different capabilities which are required by our strategy being developed or acquired?

- Is the desired emphasis on each of the various product/ market efforts being followed?

- Are our strategic conclusions about product and market projects reflected in operating plans and budgets?

- Are our incentive systems reinforcing the desired strategic direction?

- What evidence or "early warning signals" indicate that a desired financial result will, or will not, occur?

- Are there any indications that strategic priorities are upsetting operational requirements?

- How do we know that people down the line understand and support the vision?

To answer these questions, key indicators of success or performance measures must be established.

How do you determine which key indicators must be in place to ensure that your strategy is being implemented?

BOB LENTZ: At Huntington Bancshares, we make a transition in strategy from corporate to area level and then to specific profit centers. Detailed product and market actions, key assumptions, and resource requirements are noted. As each succeeding level does its strategic planning, managers are asked, "Given what you have said about your strategic plans and actions, how will you measure and monitor results?"

This can be a quantitative measure, such as the percentage increase in the number of accounts as a standard to measure loan growth. Or this can be a qualitative measure, such as customer satisfaction as measured by market survey.

We force managers to identify key measures of success and get very specific about how they measure strategic accomplishment.

LIEVEN GEVAERT: For Consumers Packaging's glass division, quality measures are critical. We compete against non-glass packages. As we get closer to the customer with our Markets-Served strategy, we see that his quality standards are being raised dramatically. We have got to make lighter and stronger glass containers, with a zero defect level. Glass weight, breakage, and defect standards are ever tighter. A bottle which weighed nine ounces five years ago is now at eight ounces.

Meeting and improving these quality standards are

essential for our glass division if we are going to be the preferred package for our customers.

How do you review strategic performance against a key indicator of success?

PETER BARTON: All capital projects above a relatively small amount must come to Varity's corporate appropriations committee for approval. The first question the committee asks is "How does this project tie in with the strategic objectives of the corporation?"

One of our strategic objectives is to increase the percentage of business which is not dependent on agriculture. Take as an example our engines division. It serves the industrial and automotive markets, as well as our agricultural group.

Suppose Perkins Engines submitted two capital appropriations, one having to do with engines for our agricultural group and one having to do with diesels for the industrial market. We at corporate would have a strategic bias and would say, "All things being equal, let's put our limited resources into the diesel project. Strategically, that is where we want to go."

How do you set key indicators for staff functions?

DON WEYENBERG: At Dow Corning, we measure strategic R&D effectiveness at several levels. We track every new product or new application for an existing product for the first five years. We look at total numbers. In the 1960s, 25 percent of our sales came from products less than six years old. This declined in the seventies. Now, we're nearly back to 20 percent.

There are ways we can measure the effectiveness of our commercialization process, from initial idea through to taking the product to market. We must reduce the length of that process and have set standards to do so. We also look at the quality of the new products and at how innovative they are.

What are sources for key indicators?

LEE SHOBE: We have found the future-opportunities matrix to be a key source for establishing Dow Chemical's key indicators of success. We have established clear accountability and are monitoring progress toward the product differentiation coming from our matrix.

These measures tell us whether or not the strategy is a success. If we don't achieve profitable sales in the high-priority cells in the matrix, we're just kidding ourselves, especially since that's where the bulk of our money is being spent.

How do you measure the profitability of strategic product and market actions?

CHET MARKS: At Dow Chemical, we set up a variable contribution analysis for each cell in the matrix, using a standard format: pounds, volume, variable cost, variable resource contribution, and variable profit contribution. We did that for each cell and then added it up. It was all done on PCs. It wasn't easy, but it didn't require a mainframe to do it either.

How do you monitor external or environmental assumptions?

JOHN MILLIKEN: At Smucker, we monitor strategic external threats at the level that is closest to the customer. Last year, we held a planning meeting in which attendees came from two or three levels in the organization, including our buyers. We talked about what external threats and opportunities they saw in the fruit or packaging markets. The list they generated included alternative sweeteners, concern for calories, plastic packaging, eating out, portion control, competitive growth from imports, and the like.

We discovered two things from this list. First, it told the corporate planning committee that our heads were not in the clouds, because we had identified a very similar list. Second, it told us that people throughout the organization were sensitive to the environment around them and knew what changes should be of concern.

VITAL SIGN: CRITICAL-ISSUES MANAGEMENT

When vision is reduced to a set of concrete actions—"little chips of diamond dust," as Dennis Schwieger of Varity called them— everyone in an organization can and will work to make vision succeed. Organizations we work with focus on the identification and resolution of critical issues as a way of converting vision to action. Critical issues are those unresolved concerns that surface from setting and implementing strategy. They must be addressed for vision to succeed.

Many people are proficient at generating long lists of key issues, but they are less adept at getting things resolved. This is especially true for issues bearing on strategic matters. These issues become the grandfathers of the organization. They live on and on and are often neglected. The cynicism that inevitably follows from unresolved critical issues robs vision of its vitality.

This does not have to be. For Tim Smucker's company, identification and resolution of critical issues are built into the routine of management. This keeps vision a vital force.

> Once a month, our officers hold a one-day business meeting. We do not talk about operational issues. We review progress on our strategic critical issues and discuss what more can be done to ensure speedier resolution.
>
> Middle managers also must be aware of critical issues and contribute to their resolution. At our quarterly operational review meetings, middle managers present their results against plan. While the focus is operational, I typically begin the meeting by reviewing the corporate critical issues. Each manager who makes a presentation refers to this list whenever something he has done relates to one of the issues.
>
> In addition, we hold an annual meeting for our senior and middle managers. We devote a number of the working sessions to critical-issue success stories. For example, last year one of our critical issues was to develop new packaging for one of our product lines. This was a high-priority issue because when a customer takes our products off the supermarket shelf, this is the first test of quality.

This packaging issue required an intense, cross-functional effort that involved everyone from purchasing to technical services. It was a tremendous achievement, and at the annual meeting, this was one of the success stories we focused on.

Highlighting achievement around critical issues is an effective way of letting our employees know how well we're implementing strategy.

In addition to building critical issues into its review meeting structure, The J. M. Smucker Company also integrates them into departmental priorities. For example, each year a critical-issues grid is prepared by the administrative function. Corporate critical issues relating to the administrative function are listed down the left side, while various administrative departments are listed across the top. These include accounting, management information systems, treasury, human resources, and legal. A kind of cross-impact analysis is conducted to determine which of these departments will be involved in the resolution of each issue, and what the level of involvement will be.

Koji Hayashi described how the management of critical issues at NISSAY is built into the planning review process:

The executive committee examines each division's strategy implementation plans very carefully. These one-year divisional plans are primarily stated as critical issues and are monitored by the executive committee two or three times a year.

Issues that cut across divisions are resolved through task forces that report to the executive committee. These are cross-functional in composition and include middle managers and top divisional executives. At division level, this process is repeated for each business unit.

Critical issues provide vision with an ongoing dynamic. Each issue has its own life expectancy. Some may remain on an organization's critical-issues agenda for a long time—for example, strategic competitive moves, ongoing government legislation, and new technological advances. Other critical issues surface once and can be resolved—for example, obtaining a new strategic capability, phasing out a particular product/ market cell, or approving a new acquisition. As issues get resolved, new ones are added. The work of implementing and maintaining strategy is never completed.

VITAL SIGN: KEEPING VISION CURRENT

Vision must be reviewed and updated periodically; otherwise, it risks becoming yesterday's version of tomorrow, oblivious to ongoing changes in the organization's internal and external environments. The strategy review and update process checks the vital signs and keeps vision in tune with changing times. Equally important, it keeps visionary thinking at the forefront of the manager's job.

The approach to strategic review and update practiced by our organizations follows a common pattern:

- An annual strategy review focuses first on progress and problems in implementing the organization's strategy. Second, it focuses on changes in assumptions about the external environment and their implications for the strategic direction. Critical issues are updated. This annual review tends to entail a fine-tuning of the vision rather than radical change.

- The annual strategy review is held at the beginning of the planning process. Conclusions from that review provide the framework for annual plans and budgets and for the updating of long-range plans.

- A formal and detailed review of the entire strategy is held every two or three years. External and internal environmental assumptions are updated. The Driving Force, key capabilities, and the future-opportunities matrix are reassessed. New product/market projects are developed.

Bob Ware provided an overview of how The Federal Reserve Bank of Cleveland approaches the annual review and update of the bank's strategy:

> Our annual planning process begins in November with a senior management review of the critical issues. We usually focus on a couple of critical issues and try to reach initial consensus on how to deal with them. Our aim is to provide some direction for the annual planning process, which begins in January.
>
> We also look at our strategy and ask, "Is there any major change that would cause us to modify or change it?" For example, given Gramm-Rudman pressure and turnover in the Board of Governors in Washington, we feel the environment in which we operate is much more cost driven. We need to be focused on how we are going to deal with that. Does this suggest a change in our Driving Force? If the answer is yes, we'll have to schedule time for a full-scale examination of the strategy, and then change our operating plans accordingly. If we decide that we can continue with the same vision and Driving Force despite the Gramm-Rudman kind of environment, then it provides the input to our planning process.

A CONCLUDING WORD

When the vital signs of vision are healthy, vision becomes a strong, accurate, vibrant guide for long-range planning and day-to-day operations. For this to happen, *vision must be managed* as thoughtfully and vigorously as operations.

Managing is working through people to achieve results. Without widespread participation from the boardroom to the plant floor, vision will belong to someone else. It will never be "ours" unless we can put the power of people behind the organization's vision.

CHAPTER V
Strategy and Participation

STRATEGY IS A TEAM SPORT. THE QUARTERBACK MAY ORCHESTRATE VISION, but it takes the whole team to win. Strategy succeeds in an organization only when there is broad, varied, and deep participation. How else do you achieve the alignment toward vision and sense of teamwork that are necessary to move forward together?

We have in previous chapters discussed and illustrated special applications of the strategy process, while indirectly attesting to the critical nature of participation. Here we will more directly discuss and illustrate the nature and importance of strategic participation, as well as the various roles people play in setting and implementing strategy.

Other than the nice warm feelings that come from participation, what are the benefits?

ZUHEIR SOFIA: Frankly, nice feelings are useless in themselves. Banking today is sailing in uncharted waters. Competition is different. Traditional answers no longer hold. This means we need as many people as possible creatively thinking about better ways. This can be done only if they are free to participate—and the place to start is with the strategy of the organization. I'm not saying that the strategy of Huntington Bancshares is or should be set by everyone. But how the strategy relates to a specific function or job can and should be thought through by the people involved.

How do you make sure that the focus provided by strategy does not inhibit the creative potential of those who participate in the strategic process?

DENNIS SCHWIEGER: At Varity's tractor division in England, we occasionally accuse our Toronto management of asking us to look for a single, magical solution. Somehow strategy got identified with being a kind of diamond hidden in an obscure place, a magical solution to be searched for.

Strategy is not a large, single, fifty-carat diamond. It is really more like flecks of diamond dust, little chips here and there. Everybody in the organization can find them. They're not the sole property of the president, or the chairman, or the directors. They're for every engineer who works on a design board, everyone who works in the shops. Everyone in the company can pick up a fleck of diamond dust.

If the effort to implement strategy is a collective one, you'll end up with a pile of diamond dust and flecks that is fifty carats in weight. That's as good as, if not better than, a diamond! If everyone knows what the strategy is, then each one should be prepared to start looking for a fleck of diamond dust in all the dirt that he sifts through every day on the job.

For example, our strategy says, first, that we are going to sell farm tractors and related farm machinery to farmers worldwide. Second, we will sell farm tractors to customer groups who can use a vehicle with properties similar to those of a tractor.

We spent a good deal of time communicating the strategy and then involving employees at every level in applying the strategy to their functions. One of our salesmen said, "Wait a minute! Given our strategy, what about selling to the airport market? Airlines need the draft capacity of a tractor to move airplanes and baggage." That salesman's question put us into a new market segment. That's a fleck of diamond dust!

Since setting strategy is a creative act, how do you stimulate that creativity?

KEIGO KOSAKA: When Fuji Photo Film divisions formulate strategy, we make sure that all the appropriate people are involved. That is, there is a balance of technical expertise, a representation of the different functions within the divisions, and a balance of personalities—those who are conservative versus the risk takers. Sometimes, we bring managers from different divisions to the strategy formulation sessions to add a wave of creativity and excitement to a quiet pond. We call this "destructive creativity."

What is the responsibility of senior executives in making sure that everyone participates in the vision?

MOTOHIRO TAKAYA: At the beginning of each fiscal year, top management at Kawasaki Steel talks very specifically to all managers about the overall strategic guidelines that have been developed up and down the organization. Every manager then develops his short-term, annual plan with the strategy as a guide. Each quarter, top management and each succeeding level of management review the overall strategy and monitor the short-term results and plans against that strategy.

   Beyond the management level, our section or business unit managers involve all of the supervisors and staff workers, such as engineers and computer programmers. These staff personnel then communicate the strategy to the blue-collar workers, thereby getting involvement at the lowest levels.

FRANK WOBST: At Huntington Bancshares, participation did not stop with the top team. We took the next level down, and instead of telling them, "This is the vision, like it or not," we said, "Top management reviewed the various options, and here is the vision we thought was most appropriate and here are the reasons why." We then allowed them to debate it and to consider other options. We thought this group should have input to the formulation of the strategy and have the opportunity to buy into it through their own involvement.

At the next level, we had ten or twelve task forces that were organized around our major businesses. Membership included middle managers. We gave them specific assignments and put them to work. For example, we asked the retail-business task force to examine and make recommendations on which products and which markets within the retail business we should be emphasizing and deemphasizing.

Once the task forces presented their conclusions to the top team for discussion and approval, the future scope and emphasis of products and markets were set. They made a fundamental contribution to the bank's future strategy.

Participation in the task forces also sharpened the focus of the managers involved, because they did a significant amount of research before they could reach conclusions. Because of all the fact gathering, analysis, and discussion, middle managers have a thorough grasp of our strategy and the environment in which it is being implemented.

How can participation help at a time of great strategic transition?

GERRY KAVANAGH: Consumers Packaging had a dramatic change in strategy, one that put significant emphasis on the plastics end of the business. My initial reaction was to be suspicious. As far as I was concerned, "plastic containers" were just bad words. We thought we were going to be in glass for the rest of our lives.

As a result of my participation in the implementation of strategy, my thinking broadened significantly. I discovered there's another world out there, the very real world of plastics. And plastics, not just glass, need to be part of our future.

So, participation can overcome resistance to strategic change. Does this lead to commitment?

ZUHEIR SOFIA: There has been a good deal of publicity around getting workers to commit operationally to quality improvements, better work methods, and the like. Commitment to strategy frequently is overlooked. One sure test of strategic commitment comes when you decide to phase out of a business because it doesn't fit your strategic profile. Getting managers from that business to commit to such a conclusion is a big challenge.

For example, until this year, we had a pay-by-phone service at Huntington Bancshares. Instead of paying bills in person, you would pick up the phone and direct an operator or a computer to pay your bills. The business did not meet our strategic expectations, so we needed to shift resources accordingly.

Participation really pays off handsomely in phaseout situations like the phone service. Through their work on the task forces, managers had an opportunity to make inputs to the strategy. As a result of the market research and discussions within each task force, these managers saw the good news and bad news unfolding. When senior management made the final decision on phaseout, no one was surprised or upset, not even the first-line officers.

What's the payoff of broad strategic participation?

ROGER AHRENS: As the production inventory and control manager at the OTC Group, I sat with the plant superintendent and the managers of manufacturing and engineering and asked, "Now that we understand the new corporate strategic direction, how should this affect our operations? What do we have to do to support the strategy?"

One of our conclusions was that, given the strategy, we would have to manufacture primarily along product lines. That had a big impact on my job. Instead of being the production inventory control manager for the whole division, I now would be managing a smaller segment of the business as we began to focus on those product groupings.

Participating in the discussions about strategy and helping to assess the impact on operations made my job change easier to take. Without that participation, there's no way I would have understood the change.

BOB ELLIS: Another benefit is that participation in the strategic process helps develop middle managers for future responsibility. In my job as director of human resources at Smucker's, developing strategic thinking skills is an important concern. It is essential for a manager's future growth and responsibility that he be exposed to strategy early on.

BEN GOODMAN: At Consumers Packaging, one of the indirect benefits of participating in the implementation of strategy was the opportunity it gave senior management to evaluate the growth potential of middle managers. I participated with a group of twelve managers in one facet of the implementation effort. This was an entirely different environment for me. Senior managers had a chance to assess our communications skills, our ability to think creatively and conceptually. Although I am still at my old job as director of distribution for container and closure products, at least two members of our team moved on to greater responsibilities.

Have you found ways to improve strategic participation?

ALLAN NIGHTINGALE: Much of the structure of our work with Kepner-Tregoe was carried into our next internal strategic effort on "Courtaulds Textile Group 2000." First, we remained Products Offered in direction. Second, the participative process was invaluable—involving the entire top team at group level and following the same concept at business unit level. In the "CTG2000" effort, we didn't start with a general environmental survey. Rather, we had a very detailed analysis of the market over the last fifteen years. Full participation was still critical, but various opinions could be bounced off a pretty hard data base.

There is plenty of "diamond dust" that can be discovered everywhere when an organization encourages participation in its vision. Both an obvious function and a subtle function are served by strategic participation. The obvious benefits include gaining commitment for the vision, helping to further refine top management's strategy, testing strategic assumptions, ensuring that strategy is not overwhelmed by operations, and unlocking the organization's creative potential.

The more subtle benefits include providing senior management with an opportunity to assess the future potential of the next generation of leaders, broadening the perspective of managers down the line so that change is more tolerable, and adding a strategic dimension to the thinking of middle managers at an early stage in their career.

THE NATURE OF STRATEGIC PARTICIPATION

To illustrate the nature of strategic participation, let us see how several of our organizations achieved broad-based involvement during two critical steps in the strategic process: developing and using the future-opportunities matrix, and reality-testing the strategic conclusions.

How do you get participation in the future-opportunities matrix?

KEIGO KOSAKA: After setting strategy in the graphic systems division of Fuji Photo Film, a broad base of managers and staff formed an implementation committee. Smaller groups of middle managers were assigned to product/market pairs coming from the future-opportunities matrix. Each month, they made a progress report to the implementation committee. All members of the committee knew the progress of our implementation efforts. This involvement continues to ensure everyone's commitment.

ZUHEIR SOFIA: At Huntington Bancshares, the future-opportunities matrix that evolved from the Driving Force was developed by task forces of senior and middle managers. Take our retail business task force as one example. We segmented that market into upscale, middle-income, and lower-income customers. But the task force concluded that the retail segment involves many services. So we set up task forces to analyze those services. One task force focused on credit. One credit product is short-term loans. Based on the criteria for emphasis, the credit task force concluded that the upscale market segment should be given a medium emphasis on this product in the short term. It will be higher over time. The lower-income market segment was given a zero emphasis for short-term loans. Recommendations such as these from all the task forces were submitted to senior management and then adopted.

KERRY KILLINGER: When the top team at Washington Mutual Financial Group set strategy, we agreed on the broad range of financial services we would offer now and on those we might consider offering in the future. This was in keeping with our Markets-Served direction.

We let this settle in for a while, then reconvened the original small group of executives, as well as a much broader group of middle managers. We wanted them to work through the issues involved in developing the future-opportunities matrix and to assign specific priorities to each cell.

Having a common, focused point of view about our future product and market emphasis is critical. But this doesn't mean anyone felt constricted. There is opportunity within our strategy for our people to be as creative as they want to be. As they participated in the process, the opportunities within the strategy took their breath away.

How do you get participation in reality-testing?

CHET MARKS: At The Dow Chemical Company we brought in every management-level employee connected with our polystyrene and polyethylene businesses. We also brought in our professional engineers, who were reasonably far up the professional ladder. We explained the process and presented the broad business strategy developed thus far. Then we said, "This is what the polyethylene and polystyrene businesses are all about. Now we want a reality test. We want you to examine the future-opportunities matrix because the segments we worked with may be too big. You may have to break a cell down into narrower products or smaller markets. We also want you to confirm this emphasis in the marketplace and give us your judgment about changes."

THE ROLES PEOPLE PLAY

In one sense, the strategic role everyone in the organization plays is the same. Carl Alderman of Huntington Bancshares explained that thinking strategically is an ongoing activity for him and his people:

> Now, you can't be consumed by strategy every minute of the day. But strategy is not a once-a-year activity. How many managers mumble, "Oh, hell, here I go again. It's time for strategic planning. God, I can't wait to get that over with!" The thought process that goes on during the concentrated period of time when strategy is being set must continue in everyone's head on a regular basis. You have to think in a strategic fashion about what you are doing.

Koji Hayashi of NISSAY commented on the commonality of strategic roles in Japan:

> In Japan, vision is not only the concern of the top people. Everyone owns the same vision, from the top to the bottom of the organization. Even when operational business is the issue, people are thinking strategically.
>
> In other countries, you often hear "This is not my responsibility" or "This is outside my job." In Japan, people recognize their basic responsibilities, but they try to broaden their contribution by thinking about what has to be done to support the vision. For example, Mr. Kinoshita is a supervisor who reports to me. But he always thinks as if he were in my position. He thinks and does what is needed to implement the strategy of the organization.

In another sense, responsibilities and roles for vision differ. Based on the experiences of our organizations, we can begin to understand who plays what role in the strategic process. First, we will consider the strategic role of the CEO; next, the roles of senior and middle managers; then the role of first-level employees; and, finally, the role of planners in the strategic process.

The Strategic Role of the CEO

Overall, the CEO is the conscience of the organization's strategy. He is part visionary, part standard-bearer, part cheerleader, and part taskmaster. He is the embodiment of the organization's vision.

CEOs who are effective visionaries know that their most important responsibilities and roles are future directed. Bob Morison of Consumers Packaging contrasted his strategic role with his short-term, operational role:

> The CEO's power is limited. As CEO of Consumers, I cannot do anything about what is happening in any of the plants today, tomorrow, next week, next month, probably the next two or three months. This is true because we are a fair-sized company, and you don't just turn the tap on and off. A key to my role is concerning myself with the future health and prosperity of the corporation. This means I must take a longer-term view than the people who are charged with day-to-day responsibilities. I must look further out, set a direction, and meet whatever challenges come along to the future of this business.

Victor Rice of Varity stated with vigor the CEO's unique responsibility for achieving vision:

> You hear a lot these days about "consensus management." Frankly, I don't believe there is a consensus manager in the entire Western world. Yes, there are different management styles, but they only represent different ways for getting the organization to follow the CEO's vision.
> In the final analysis, the CEO establishes the vision and constantly pushes it. He may, in the process, gather the judgments of those around him. But, ultimately, he is the one responsible for saying, "This is the way we're going!"

Allan Nightingale of Courtaulds Fabrics Group believes in participation but knows that, in the last analysis, the strategy is his:

At the end of the day, the strategy rests with the "gut feel" of the chief executive. He is the focal point of vision. When he is in his office with the door shut, and everybody has had their input, it's what he feels about vision that matters. Strategy setting is not a fully democratic process. It is democratic in that everyone has his say, but then the boss says, "This is where we're going." It's got to be like that. Participation provides for dissecting, forming, sharpening, and polishing the chief executive's vision in the first place. What he ends up with is what really matters.

The CEOs we have worked with feel they have primary responsibility for:
- *Articulating the vision.* Strategy begins in the mind and heart of the CEO. He must get out what is inside him so that it can be debated, tested, and enriched by the key people around him.

The process of articulating vision entails finesse on the part of the CEO. Dictating the vision may get compliance, but rarely commitment. Sometimes, the best approach is to give the top team enough rope to prove themselves, as Lou Pepper, the CEO of the Washington Mutual Financial Group, implied:

We broke into two subgroups to consider the question "How should we determine the products we should sell, the markets we should sell into, and the emphasis that should be given to these products and markets?" The discussion in both groups was lengthy. I quietly took an easel, slipped into the hallway, and wrote down the criteria that I always keep in mind when making strategic decisions. When I was done, I went back into the room to listen to the summary reports from each group. They had almost everything I had noted down, although the language was slightly different. I then shared my thinking with them.

When you set strategy and discover that everyone on the top team is using the same standards, that builds mutual confidence. Besides, making your thinking visible certainly beats the perception that your strategic decision making is based on an "eenie, meenie, minie, moe" approach.

- *Ensuring internal strategic consistency.* It is not always possible or even desirable to have a single vision dominate every facet of the organization. Yet, given all the complexity, an organization can easily become a house divided. The CEO ensures that each major area of the business first has a strategic vision, and that this is consistent with the overall corporate thrust. Varity Corporation's Victor Rice elaborated:

> We are now in the process of dividing the company into a number of businesses. Each business had an idea of its own strategic direction. Then, we set our corporate direction and asked each of our businesses to take another hard look at its direction to ensure consistency. As long as the strategies of the individual businesses are compatible with the corporate direction, I'll be satisfied that the company is moving forward together. We will eventually wind up with a number of businesses, each with its own identity in support of the corporation.

- *Establishing strategic reward mechanisms.* This responsibility represents a tough challenge. The CEO makes sure that key people are rewarded, not only for quarter-by-quarter operational performance, but also for longer-term strategic performance. This means looking at reward systems both strategically and operationally, and delineating the relevant accomplishments and rewards for each. In terms of strategic rewards, simplicity is a real virtue. Gordon Gund of Gund Investment Corporation observed:

> As CEO, one of my tasks is to make sure that the senior executives remain focused on the strategy. One way to do this is to tie the reward structure to strategic performance. At the beginning of each year, I sit down with each senior executive and establish strategic and operational objectives.
>
> We distinguish two kinds of strategic objectives. One is related to the fulfillment of strategic goals here at corporate. For example, when we set strategy, we identify the critical issues necessary for successfully implementing the

strategy. These issues are converted into performance objectives for each senior manager.

The other type of strategic objective relates to the top operating management out in the field. We want to make sure they and their subordinates achieve the strategic goals for their units. For example, one goal might relate to how well our field managers communicate the strategy to middle managers and how well they tie the job of middle managers to the strategy.

• *Involving the board of directors.* While the relationship between a CEO and his board of directors will vary, it is the unique responsibility of the CEO to communicate his organization's vision to the board and gain the board's commitment and support. Bob Morison of Consumers Packaging described the process:

> The board of directors should agree on the broad policy perspectives of the corporation, that is, the long-term strategy of the company as presented by the management. There must be a mutuality of understanding and of respect between the board and management. As long as the board realizes it cannot manage the company, and as long as management understands it isn't going to set the long-term objectives of the company on its own, you have an unbeatable combination.

• *Communicating the vision.* In addition to the board, the CEO plays an important role in communicating the strategy to other important stakeholders, such as stockholders and employees, and to important public sectors, such as the financial community, government entities, and the like. (See Chapter 6.)

• *Keeping the strategy relevant.* Nothing is forever. Not even the most incisive vision can remain as is. A good pilot flies ahead of his plane, and, likewise, the CEO is out in front of his organization's strategy. He pushes for ongoing updates of the strategy to ensure that the vision he and his key people have articulated remains the best bet for the future. This is how Jack Ludington of Dow Corning viewed it:

You have to be able to say to a senior manager, "Well, John, you're right. You do have a unique situation. It doesn't quite fit with the corporate strategy, but it probably fits very well with your own product strategy. Go to it." As the CEO, I do not want to be surrounded with clones, but with people who can do things differently, provided they share the same basic vision of the future as the rest of us.

It's amazing how little change there is in the big strategic issues. A lot of tweaking of the strategy takes place. You may have to fine-tune the strategy by making a 10-degree adjustment, but rarely do you have to pound your head against a wall and change things 180 degrees.

As you proceed from strategy to tactics, you're in trouble if you cannot be flexible. You'll never develop a strategy that is going to be absolutely right on course. You must plan for adjustments and allow for the unique situation.

The Strategic Role of Senior Executives

The senior management team is the strategic alter ego of the CEO. As Ned Richardson of The Federal Reserve Bank of Cleveland defined it:

> My responsibilities as vice-president of service management include helping to formulate the strategy and then motivating, pushing, shoving, coaxing, and cajoling so that the strategy gets implemented.

The senior executives with whom we have worked assume these responsibilities:

• *Helping articulate the strategic vision.* Senior managers are in the positions they occupy because the CEO values their thinking and contributions. They owe him candor, their best advice, and a corporate perspective. They are there to challenge and sharpen the CEO's strategic vision. This is the moment for loyal opposition. No matter how deep the debate along the way, the end product of their labor should be a clear, simple, and specific vision that merits their commitment. According to Larry Reed of Dow Corning:

> The role of the chief operating officer is to challenge and then support the chief executive officer's view of what has to be done, and then ensure that the organization is actually doing it. Both are responsible for working with other members of the top team to define what the company should be doing in the future, and all should be sure that the vision is consistent with the interest of the shareholders. I personally spent much time on the strategy statement, agonizing over every word. We redid the statement a number of times until it precisely expressed what all of us on the top team believed.

• *Ongoing commitment and support.* Once vision is formulated, senior managers provide demonstrated support for it. They guide efforts to further refine and test the strategy as it applies to their areas of responsibility. They make sure that vision cuts deeply into their respective operations by having their strategy, structure, plans, and budgets carry the mark of the overall vision. They provide opportunities for broad participation in implementation efforts so that the top team's strategy becomes "our vision." Like the CEO, they, too, are champions of the strategy and take every opportunity to explain the strategy, solicit comments about it, and make it apply to their operation. They help make the vision come alive. Ned Richardson of The Federal Reserve Bank of Cleveland said it this way:

> Ensuring the complete understanding of the strategy and its implications for our operations is something we live and breathe every day. The definition and clarity of our vision have enhanced our ability to communicate it. Our staff knows that the strategy is everyone's marching orders. Their challenge is to implement it proficiently. Our job is to reinforce the message day in and day out. I don't think you will find many people out there asking, "What's the bank's vision?" My function is intricately related to the planning process, because we create the planning documents. We're the major cheerleaders for strategy.

• *Setting strategic priorities and managing strategically.* The act of setting and implementing strategy raises top-priority issues which must be resolved for strategy to become a reality. The senior managers from the organizations we have worked with ensure that the critical strategic issues relevant to their end of the business get addressed on a timely basis. They see to it that strategy gets its share of time and attention in the face of competing operational demands. In addition, senior managers make sure that the decisions made within their area, from resource allocation to capital expenditure to compensation, reflect strategic as well as operational criteria.

John Milliken discussed how he helps keep strategic priorities at the forefront at Smucker's:

> I keep a calendar in which I note the strategic issues I'm responsible for during a particular year. I don't have to wonder. They're right in front of me. These issues are my strategic performance objectives. Where appropriate, I translate them further for my subordinates.
>
> We all know what the priorities are—both strategic and operational. My subordinates will challenge me if I give them a task that does not support our strategy. They'll tell me, "That's not strategic. It's off course. It's not on plan." So I know they're managing their people and their own time like that as well.

The Strategic Role of Middle Managers

In most organizations, the great black hole of strategic involvement is the middle-management tier that includes key business unit managers, functional managers, managers of geographical areas, staff department heads, and key individual contributors. This black hole need not exist, as Dow Chemical's Chet Marks indicated:

> One of the most trite comments that you hear today in corporations comes from folks who say, "I am only a middle manager and nobody tells me anything." Or "I am

not in the power loop, so I can't have an impact on the corporation." There's an endless series of excuses.

Every manager at every level in every size of company is a manager of something. People who manage small businesses, or functions, or small geographical regions don't have the same size job as people who manage big businesses or large geographical areas. But they have similar strategic responsibilities.

They have a responsibility for setting a strategic direction. It helps them immensely if a hierarchy of strategies comes down through the organization to give them guidance. But if nobody tells them what to do strategically, they should decide what they will do and communicate up to their superiors and down to their subordinates. If your superiors don't like what you're doing, they'll tell you not to do it. If they do, maybe you'll be promoted.

Motohiro Takaya of the Kawasaki Steel Corporation believes that middle managers in Japan play an essential role in the strategic process:

> We encourage all of our managers to think as if they were all presidents of their own companies. For example, top executives at the iron factory develop very broad strategic guidelines. These are further refined at divisional level and sent to the section manager. These section or business unit managers develop detailed strategies for their units, which are sent back up to division level. Each of the division managers further refines strategy at his level and coordinates his conclusions with those of the other division managers. The overall division strategy is then sent back up to the senior executives, who refine the factory strategy accordingly. Of course, there are iterations at each step, but this is the typical approach in Japanese industry.

Our organizations encourage middle managers to contribute to, challenge, and critique the strategy set at the next level up. But when the strategic baton is passed to managers at business unit, functional, and geographical levels, their responsibility is to understand that vision and make it work. Here is how those we work with at middle-management levels define their strategic responsibilities:

• *Understanding the strategy.* Middle managers are responsible for understanding the vision and all the nuances that apply to their function. They will impair implementation efforts without this thorough understanding and commitment to where the organization is headed. This is a proactive responsibility. If the vision is unclear, or if information that is needed to implement the vision is inadequate, these managers take the initiative to probe for answers at the next level up.

• *Further detailing and implementing the corporate strategy.* In many instances, middle managers further specify a section of the corporate future-opportunities matrix for study and then develop specific action plans. Some managers are responsible for developing or acquiring a particular capability required by the strategy. Others are responsible primarily for surveillance of how well the strategy is being implemented, or of customers' perceptions, or of the assumptions underlying the strategy. Still others are responsible for seeing that systems are in place to support and monitor the strategic direction. While middle managers have different roles in implementing strategy, one connecting thread is the shared responsibility for effectively communicating strategy to subordinates.

Malcolm Vinnicombe of Courtaulds Fabrics Group spoke about detailing the corporate strategy at the middle-management level:

> I'm talking about the ten units which make up profit centers, which in turn constitute a division. Understanding the relative emphasis of different products or markets as defined by our corporate strategy was immensely useful at unit level. At this level, we had all the facts and could actually further refine top management's product and market thinking as it applied to our area of the business.
>
> For example, we asked, "What's the future of 45-inch nylon for linings for Marks and Spencer?" [a London-based retail chain] While we believed we were doing quite a lot of business in that area, we actually weren't. It was

shrinking, not growing. That buildup of information enabled us to look at trends against the strategy and ask, "What do we want to do in five or ten years?"

• *Information gathering.* How viable is the vision when looked at from the narrower perspective of a middle manager's job? Middle managers and key contributors are closest to the action and are top management's best sources of information, whether that information tests assumptions that underlie the strategy or indicates how well strategy implementation efforts are proceeding. Providing this information may involve the marketing and sales functions in testing customer intentions and reactions, as well as competitive moves. It may involve research, product design, and engineering in verifying product requirements. Finance, management information systems, and accounting may be required to provide the appropriate performance measures. Personnel, training, and human-resource groups may provide information on levels of commitment and strategic understanding.

The Strategic Role at First Levels

To the average employee down the line, an organization tends to be little more than matter in motion, a place without larger context. As John Dewey, the American philosopher, observed, for many workers, earning one's living is not living one's life.

But Shigeo Iiyama demonstrates that at Fuji Photo Film, the average worker performs as though he were indeed living his life:

Everyone, including blue-collar workers, participates in implementing strategy. We have a system in place encouraging all employees to make suggestions for product modifications and innovations that will support our strategic emphasis. If the person who makes a suggestion wants to undertake the project himself, the company will give him money to do the job. This system makes blue-collar workers feel that they are part of strategy implementation. The real worth of all employees is the worth of the head and not the body.

Ed Lowell of the OTC Group made the same point as Shigeo Iiyama, but from an American perspective:

> It is absolutely essential that people feel that they are contributing to the vision. We take pains to ensure that our people, from the shop floor right on up, understand where they fit in the whole process and that their role is important. To be flexible, to be responsible, to do quality work, people have to understand that they are an important part of the organization. If they understand the vision, the end products they are working on, and the importance of their contribution, they will be responsive, work toward higher quality, and reduce costs. They'll do that in spades.

Vision does not stop at managerial and supervisory ranks. Here is how our organizations see their responsibilities at the employee level:

• *Understanding the strategy.* First-level personnel do not require the same depth of strategic understanding as higher-level managers. But they should have sufficient understanding to realize the benefits of working in an organization which integrates day-to-day operational activities with the longer-term success promised by the vision. Tim Smucker cited an example that demonstrates the payoff from that understanding:

> Typically, I arrive at a plant a little early, before the formal strategy/operations review. I try to meet informally with as many plant people as I can.
>
> Once, I sat beside a woman and asked her how long she had been with us and what shift she worked on. It turned out she had been with us for seven years and worked on the night shift. I next said to her, "It's only two-thirty in the afternoon. Why did you come in for this meeting?"
>
> Her reply was "I wouldn't have missed this meeting for

the world. I want to know what the company is doing, and I appreciate being included."

• *Seeing the "fit."* Employees at grass-roots levels should be able to relate their jobs and priorities to the overall strategy. Achieving quality standards on the assembly line may be the critical factor in product differentiation that makes a Products-Offered strategy succeed. At the sales level, taking time with the customer to probe for new needs can be critical to a Markets-Served strategy. At technician level, in the research function, staying on top of the relevant literature might just provide the key to keeping the Technology Driving Force on the leading edge.

Lee Shobe of The Dow Chemical Company explained that his strategic plans typically involve people right down to the "doer" level:

> Our sales force has an account roster for sales calls. Annual account plans require the salesman to assess an account in terms of purchase potential, actual purchases, status of the relationship, new development programs, anticipated man-days with the account, levels of technical development and support, management time needed, and any other major resource requirements. His action plans over the year for any account will be very clear and have strategic emphasis.

The Strategic Role of the Planning Function

Chet Marks commented insightfully about the role of the planning function:

> I think a planner ought to understand and teach strategic thinking. I don't plan anybody's business for them. I try to create an environment in which managers know what needs to be done and can execute it themselves. As the director of planning and new venture development for the plastics group of Dow Chemical in the United States, I spend at least half my time trying to make sure that the

plastics businesses have a coherent strategy, and that we are on the way to implementing that strategy.

No organization we have worked with delegates strategy setting to planners. Vision cannot be delegated to consultants either inside or outside the organization. After all, how can anyone else dictate what *your* vision should be? This extends to implementation as well. Every organization we write about views strategy implementation as the responsibility of management down the line.

Does this leave no role for the planning function in the strategic process? As Chet Marks implied, the planning function can play a crucial role in facilitating strategic efforts. In some organizations, this means that planning participates with the top team in setting strategy. In other organizations, it means the planning function acts as a stimulus for vision, alerting the top management team to significant new threats or opportunities that require a strategic reassessment. Planning also provides the necessary formats, steps, and procedures to get strategy implemented. It assists key executives in communicating the overall vision so that it becomes relevant to all areas of the business. In their strategic role, planners assess, challenge, support, coordinate, and instruct.

A CONCLUDING WORD

People make vision happen. Strategic "diamond dust" is everywhere. To find it, each person must understand and act on his role in either formulating, testing, implementing, or monitoring vision.

Strategy, we said at the outset of this chapter, is a team sport. When the entire team does not know the play, the quarterback usually gets sacked. Then everyone loses. Communication is essential.

CHAPTER VI

Communicating Vision Through the Ranks

ONCE UPON A TIME, AND NOT TOO LONG AGO, THERE WAS A WIDELY SHARED perception that strategy was the exclusive preserve of the CEO and a few of his trusted subordinates. Only after a major business decision had been made would others in the organization get a glimmer of the organization's direction. Few knew for sure whether or not that direction was well conceived. The rest were left hoping for the best. Such uncertainty produced strategic restlessness in quite a few organizations. You cannot commit to, take advantage of, or be guided by what you do not know or only vaguely perceive.

Things have changed, at least in the organizations we know. Vision is no longer hidden in the vest pockets of a few executives. It is being brought into the open, communicated in a tangible way so everyone can grab hold of the vision and work together for its implementation. But negotiating your way through the subject of communicating vision can be like driving through a maze. The odds of staying on course are slim without a plan of attack. Our plan has four facets:

1. The need to communicate vision

2. The five basic principles of effective strategic communication

3. Mediums for the strategic message

4. Who needs to know what

THE NEED TO COMMUNICATE VISION

Communicating vision—is this just another fad wrapped up in fine words?

CHET MARKS: Not at Dow Chemical. We needed to explain how we arrived at our vision in sufficient detail so our people could understand the logic behind our conclusions, as well as their place in the process. We wanted to explain what we did and at the same time have our conclusions accepted. We accomplished that by making it obvious that the people who developed the strategy knew how and why they did it, and were committed to its success. People down the line will commit to almost anything if they see that top management knows what it is doing and there is logic behind its thinking.

If communicating vision is so important, how do you make it stick down the line?

JOHN TACHENY: One way we at the Truth Division of the OTC Group make vision stick is by writing things down. Whenever we want our engineering staff to work on a problem, we complete a project authorization form and pass it along to our engineers. As a result of going through the strategic process, we display the future-opportunities matrix on each form. This way, the engineers know immediately what the importance of the problem is.

Another way to make strategy stick is to have customer standards that stem from the strategy. Before we set strategy, a good customer would get any product he wanted. Other customers—ones we did not know as well— did not get as much time from our design engineers, or our model shop, or our marketing people.

Now that we have a strategy—and one which has been widely communicated—people know why we should bend over backwards to help a particular client. It is by strategic design. Strategy told us why.

What happens when the implications of vision for an operation are more negative than positive?

TIM SMUCKER: At Smucker's, when a division, a market center, or a product area does not fit our strategy, it is best to address the issue with the manager in charge. Some of our best managers are in problem areas. We would talk with them and ask for ideas about the best ways to get out of that particular operation.

This involves a delicate approach to communications. It could produce a lot of unnecessary anxiety down in the organization. There is no substitute for taking the managers of the group which is to be phased out and asking them, "Can you help us address this problem?"

On balance, what difference does communicating vision really make?

ROBERT MORRISON: Looking back over the years, having a clear strategy—and communicating it—produced a total focus or consensus among J. M. Smucker's top management. This, in turn, filtered down to the middle managers and throughout the organization.

This total "mind-fix" makes my job easier. When we sit down each year to do our planning and budgeting, there are no surprises. There is no guesswork about where we are going over the long term. Everyone knows what the focus and emphasis of our planning should be.

GORDON GUND: My experience with the companies in the Gund Investment Corporation has been that when senior management embraces and clearly communicates the strategy, middle management, in turn, communicates the strategy equally well. This gives everyone in the organization a better sense of how their tasks fit into the greater vision. Knowing that we are not just performing a repetitive task without larger meaning is important to each one of us. When you contribute to a common strategic goal, you feel a great sense of accomplishment.

THE FIVE BASIC PRINCIPLES OF EFFECTIVE STRATEGIC COMMUNICATION

We have observed these essential components for effectively communicating vision:

1. Common strategic language

2. Simplicity/specificity

3. Testing for understanding

4. Repetition

5. Relevance

1. Principle: A Common Strategic Language

To have a common language for vision requires a strategic process—a necessary sequence of logical steps for collecting and analyzing information and then drawing inferences. The essence of the strategic process employed by our organizations involves environmental analysis, basic beliefs, the Driving Force, thrust for future business development, future product/market scope and emphasis, reality-testing, positioning, action planning, critical issues, key indicators, and monitoring.

Ned Richardson of The Federal Reserve Bank of Cleveland observed that everyone who has been involved in this strategic process at the bank uses terms which have the same meaning:

> All of us at the bank have a clear understanding of our Driving Force and the future-opportunities matrix, as well as what the marching orders are to get us there. The strategic message is reinforced almost every day. You won't find too many people here who ask, "What's our Driving Force, our thrust for future business development, and our product/market emphasis?"

Organizations with a great number of disparate businesses, such as those driven by a Return/Profit Driving Force, reap special advantages from having a common strategic language. In such organizations, strategic unity or consistency can be difficult to achieve. Peter Barton of Varity comments on the benefits of a common language in a Return/Profit kind of setting:

> When you're dealing with an organization with different businesses, each with different objectives, there's a lot to juggle from a corporate perspective. We had a common strategic process and language at the corporate level and

rolled this into each business. Our divisional vice-presidents understand what we're talking about when we use strategic concepts, and we at corporate can understand the businesses when they talk about their strategic objectives and action plans.

Likewise, the multinational organization has great need for a common strategic language. Dennis Schwieger of Varity's tractor division observed:

> Once we set strategy, the question was "How do we communicate it in Germany, France, Italy, and the United Kingdom, each of which has its own culture, management style, and power base?" We had to communicate the facts about our strategy, and the underlying rationale for the direction we chose, without creating resentment. To accomplish this, we trained local facilitators in each country in every aspect of the strategic process. This approach helped us to communicate the strategy internationally.

A common language as expressed in a strategic process does not provide a surefire solution to conflict, but it does help to channel discussion and debate. Kenichi Kinoshita of NISSAY commented:

> It is difficult to say *sayonara* to old thinking. The Driving Force helps us to do this. If our executives argue about various new directions, we can resolve any differences by using the concept of Driving Force. Everyone has a common language and a common frame of reference. While everyone cannot have his own way, the process leads to a common vision to which everyone can commit.

2. Principle: Simplicity/Specificity

Without much effort, strategy can become a mine field of complexity that only the gods, gurus, and a few professors can walk through and survive. For strategy to be implemented effectively, it must be kept simple so that mere mortals can readily understand and apply it. These remarks by Tim Smucker made the point:

> Whenever I ask some of my business friends about their strategy, they usually show me a three-ring binder that is six inches thick. It is full of numbers and very operational. If it addresses the question "What should the business look like in the future?" you can't find the answer.
>
> The Smucker strategy is simple and specific enough to be carried in everyone's head. If further reference is required, I can pull our ten-page strategy from my brief-case, which, incidentally, is where I always carry it.

3. Principle: Testing for Understanding

The first test of how well someone grasps the essentials of a message often comes from observing that individual's behavior. When behavior reflects the message, you know you have gotten through. Action confirms understanding. However, action also can be living proof of the failure to grasp the message. This can be a costly way to discover that the communication effort missed the mark.

A far less costly alternative involves testing a person or group's understanding of the strategy *prior* to having anyone take action. Testing for understanding means asking others to repeat the strategic message in their own words or to discuss how it would be applied to their own area, or how it would be applied to a hypothetical case example. This increases the likelihood that understanding and action will square with strategic expectations.

Testing for strategic understanding is especially important because strategic thinking often leads to actions that are quite different from business as usual. Kerry Killinger described how the Washington Mutual Financial Group subtly tested the strategic understanding of middle managers:

> We organized a communication program for middle managers with a different spin on it. First, we tried to get them to understand where top management was coming from

regarding the strategy. Then we attempted to get their buy-in to our Markets-Served Driving Force. Next, we put our middle managers through workshops in which we asked them to provide greater detail for our future-opportunities matrix. Small teams were assigned a specific product/market cell, and we asked them, using the criteria we developed for product and market emphasis, to tell us how they would set priorities. We then compared their conclusions to those reached by the top team to see if we all were on the same track. We were.

One way Larry Reed of Dow Corning tests for strategic understanding is to probe the issue of quality whenever he visits plants. He wants to know firsthand how well quality is being implemented:

I don't just talk to the managers—I also talk to the operators and ask them questions. I test their understanding of the implications for quality of our strategy. Product quality is critical to our competitive advantage, and I want to know: Are we pursuing quality in that plant at a level that is consistent with the strategic need? Are the supervisors involved enough? Is the organization involved enough?

4. Principle: Repetition

In a society with an exponential increase in the amount of knowledge available (and, perhaps, an even greater increase in the volume of advertising), information overload is a clear and present danger. Much of the information that descends on today's managers centers around operational concerns. That is as it should be, but how do you get the strategic message through that maze?

Our organizations have found that one well-worn method still works best: Repeat the message about vision as often as you can. According to Craig Blizzard of Consumers Packaging:

As we moved from a Products-Offered to a Markets-Served Driving Force, the strategic message was driven home over and over again. It had a great influence on how our group looked at things. Repeated contact and repeated discussion made the point.

Assuming that strategy is well understood could be deadly to your organization's strategic health. Repetition is a good antidote, as Smucker's Bill Boyle pointed out:

> A recent article in a business journal quoted a number of CEOs who said that you cannot repeat and reinforce your strategy enough. They felt—and so do I—that you cannot assume your employees will retain the strategic message.
>
> We have an annual planning meeting to review our strategy to a fare-thee-well. At quarterly reviews and meetings with employees, our officers continually talk about basic beliefs and our vision; we never assume that everybody knows it all. We constantly reinforce it.

From his position at Dow Corning, Larry Reed provided an effective summary on the subject of repetition:

> I've only been president of Dow Corning for a few years. If there is one thing I've learned on the subject of communicating our vision, it is the need to repeat, repeat, repeat the specifics of the strategic message. The broad brush just doesn't work.

5. Principle: Relevance

"What are the implications of vision for my area of responsibility?" Getting managers and key contributors down the line to ask this question is an important step in having them lay claim to vision. When the strategic message is perceived as both making sense and making a difference, the force of relevance is on the organization's side. And that is powerful!

"Practice what you preach" is a time-honored axiom. Regardless of what senior managers may say about the organization's vision, and how convincingly they say it, the most persuasive reinforcer of vision is tangible strategic action. It brings rhetoric to life. Kerm Campbell spoke of how he put teeth into the strategic message when he managed one of Dow Corning's business units:

> I reported back to my team about the nature of our vision. I wanted every team member to know where the corporation was going and the implications of the overall direction for our business unit.
>
> For example, one strategic objective involved changing the proportions of business from a 50/50 mix of high-volume to high-value-added products to 40 percent high-volume and 60 percent high-value-added products. This goal is getting translated into individual objectives for each member of the team.
>
> More concretely, this means reducing resources allocated to high-volume programs and increasing the resources devoted to the high-value-added side of the business. When you start making moves on resource allocation, that brings home the message about vision very dramatically.

Ed Lowell of the OTC Group bases his approach to making strategy relevant on the practical premise that education begins with the individual and where he is at a particular point in time:

> Rather than explain the theory and all the detail of strategy, I cut through the long-winded lectures and boil things down and relate them to specifics that our people handle day in and day out. These include operational excellence, just-in-time production systems, and employee involvement. For example, I take our Markets-Served Driving Force and show that operational excellence means fitting the quality level to the customer need. Our strategy and these issues all fit tightly together.

From the perspective of a long and highly successful business career, Victor Rice of Varity succinctly summarized the relevance principle:

The truth is, I'm not a young tiger anymore. As I've gotten older, I've learned one thing that you don't learn as a youngster. The only real strategic success comes when you deliver on the vision. We did far more to support our Return/Profit vision by acquiring the Dayton-Walther Corporation than by all the fancy talk and good intentions.

MEDIUMS FOR THE STRATEGIC MESSAGE

As messages move along the nerves of an organization's communications network, they can be delivered in many different ways: one-on-one discussions; formal and informal in-house meetings; press releases; the annual report and meeting; briefings to the stockholders, board of directors, and the financial community; the house organ; advertising copy; special brochures, pamphlets and memos; videotapes; monthly or quarterly review meetings; the president's letter; social events; and on and on.

There is no one best medium to express vision, and given the array of alternatives we have just enumerated, there probably is little need to invent new ones. The organizations here have found that the most effective way to move the strategy message is to use the existing communications channels, making sure the effort is well coordinated.

Toshiki Yokokawa, of the electronic components division of Oki Electronic Devices Group, described how his company used the medium of existing quality-control circles to communicate vision:

Our workers have strong concerns about strategic change. Our strategy indicated that we must be dominant in certain market segments. We wanted our workers to think about the impact of the strategy on their job responsibilities. The division manager and the section managers attended circle meetings to explain the strategy and answer any questions. This discussion flowed easily because we used a well-established meeting format.

The least effective way to communicate is to rely on the one-way, "say-and-tell" session or on a pamphlet, where there is little opportunity for participant involvement. Academic discussions about the theory or process of setting strategy are deadly. But showing how the process led to the vision and to action animates the discussion.

Pretesting the medium is a must. Put yourself in the place of the audience. Is this setting most conducive to getting the message across? Whatever the medium, those that follow the principles of communication outlined earlier in this chapter are the most effective.

Here are a series of comments that illustrate various ways to communicate the strategic message.

Formal Meetings

DURWOOD CHALKER: We held meetings with the top thirty-five people at Central and South West, who were charged with implementing an important facet of our strategy—the diversification program. Our top team presented the Driving Force and the strategy to this group and fielded questions.

We then divided the thirty-five executives into smaller groups and asked them to generate ideas for diversification within the context of the strategy. This gave participants a feeling that they were really involved. It also tested their comprehension of our strategic direction. We're investigating a number of ideas that were developed by these groups.

Informal Communication

VICTOR RICE: Every three or four months, when I'm on a trip, I go to the canteen at the site I'm visiting and sit down with the people in that business. Ostensibly, it's an update on where Varity is. Actually, it's a wonderful vehicle for getting across a bit of our strategic message and for getting feedback on what is worrying our people.

A lot of their worries often come out as questions. "What

do you think is happening to John Deere?" What our people are really asking is "Relative to John Deere, what are we going to do?" You get a terrific opportunity to discuss key issues and make the relevant strategy points in the process.

Newsletters

AL DOMAN: The first step in communicating our vision to all Washington Mutual Financial Group's employees, and probably our most significant one, is to publish a newsletter that describes what we are doing strategically. It describes the strategy and the implementation plan with plenty of examples.

The reaction has been extremely positive. Many people have said, "I now understand what senior management has been saying. Before, I only got little bits of the strategy. Now, it's starting to sink in."

Taking Advantage of Another Program

PAUL SMUCKER: We make a concerted effort to share Smucker's vision with everyone in the company, including our secretaries, and that really adds to our esprit de corps. A while ago, we held two-day training programs for our secretaries. I spoke at the beginning of the program about our strategy—what a Products-Offered strategy meant, why we adopted it, what the implications are for our products and markets.

The feedback from the secretaries was tremendous. Many of them came up to me and said, "Now I understand some of the memos coming from this office and what the company is trying to accomplish."

Multimedia Approach

GEOFF WOODS: I personally manage Courtaulds Fabrics' program to communicate strategy. I brought in an assistant just to make sure that all our communication efforts establish links between strategy and operations.

All our meetings have a strategic element built in. Each meeting begins with a progress report on our strategic implementation efforts. Whether we're talking about customer service, product design, or reviewing key accounts, we refer back to the strategy.

I edit the company newspaper. One of the objectives of the paper is to increase the understanding of our strategy. Thus far we have published seven issues aimed at this objective and have actually won an industry publishing award.

The strategic message goes not only to our people but to our customers as well. It is carried to them on all fronts, from technical to sales and service.

ZUHEIR SOFIA: The top four people at Huntington Bancshares made a videotape to describe our vision and its broad impact on the organization. First, we showed the video to all our officers and answered their questions. Then, the officers and the group heads reporting to them held a meeting with every employee in their particular group. For example, the executive vice-president for capital-market and investment banking and I met with the investment banking group, about sixty people.

I opened the meeting with why it is essential for everyone in the group to understand and apply the strategy. Next, we showed the video, and then the executive vice-president traced the implications of the overall vision for the various sections of the group. He said, "This is what the strategy means for us in the capital-market and investment banking group. It means this range of products for these types of markets."

He then outlined what the strategy meant to the individual, the changes it required, and what had to be done differently, and he explained that the strategy would be built into the group's plans.

At the end of the meeting, we distributed a brochure to each participant which summarized our strategy and made it easily accessible for planning and decision making.

WHO NEEDS TO KNOW WHAT

We have seen the various ways in which vision is transmitted down through the organization. But there are other important groups that have an essential interest in the organization's vision, and the pathways of communication must extend to them. Before we illustrate how our organizations have communicated vision to these other groups, however, a word of caution is in order. The need to fully disclose the details of vision must be balanced against the competing need to maintain confidentiality. Frequently, key aspects of the strategy must remain with a select few to avoid the risk of telegraphing strategic moves to competitors or to employees who have not been adequately prepared. This is a judgment call that must be made on a situational basis.

One pathway for communicating vision leads to the board of directors. Another extends to a newly acquired company. Other pathways lead to stockholders, to the financial community and customers, and to suppliers and distributors.

Communicating Vision to the Board of Directors

Many of our organizations require the approval of the board of directors for the strategy that management develops. Board members must understand the process and then probe and challenge the specific content of the strategy, eventually leading to any adjustment and approval. Once approved, the strategy becomes broad policy and the benchmark for future operational reviews by the board.

There are no magic formulas for approaching the board with the strategic message. Bob Morison of Consumers Packaging found that a straightforward presentation worked best:

> I made up a series of slides relating to our strategic process and talked with our board about how to cross the bridge from strategy to planning to action. I discussed our shift to a Markets-Served Driving Force and told the board that we worked with outside consultants who provided a process for setting strategy. I mentioned that we took the

strategy to the second management tier of about forty people for discussion, input, and commitment.

Had we gone to the board without first involving these forty people, we would have been vulnerable to the board asking whether or not the organization supported top management's view. Our strategy provided a vehicle for debate, discussion, and board approval.

Durwood Chalker of the Central and South West Corporation approached his board quite differently:

I have three standing committees on my board. I ran our strategy by the three committee chairmen, each of whom represents a different area of expertise. This planted the strategic direction of the corporation as top management saw it with key board members. I knew the word would spread through the board, and this facilitated getting the strategy approved.

Lou Pepper of the Washington Mutual Financial Group added "zing" to his communications with the board. His objective was to have the board put him and his top team through their strategic paces by asking the really tough questions:

I'm the only insider on our board. The rest of the board is composed of outside CEOs. They are smart and not very shy. They don't hold back anything. We presented the strategy, and they wanted to know how, precisely, we planned to achieve it. They asked the penetrating questions. What management was after was the board's toughest critique and, we hoped, its consent.

Communicating to the New Company on the Block

Richard Smucker provided an example of how to communicate vision to a newly acquired company:

Once we were convinced that Knudsen and Sons, Inc., fit our strategic profile, we sat down with the senior management team and reviewed our strategic plan with them. This was before we made the acquisition.

We showed the Knudsen executives our basic beliefs, our Driving Force statement, and the future product/market scope and emphasis. We wanted them to know what we were all about. The strategy session was very instrumental in getting Knudsen's top management to join our company. Their people could see exactly where we were headed.

Once the acquisition was made, we asked Bill Knudsen if he thought having a strategic framework for his company was important. He was very receptive to the idea, and the subsequent strategy sessions with the Knudsen top management team helped them to communicate their strategic framework to us. It helped us to see the uniqueness of the Knudsen organization.

Telling It to Customers, Stockholders, and the Financial Community

Consumers Packaging provides an illustration of how one company moved the message about its change in vision to its customers and to the financial community. Ben Goodman spoke about discussions with customers concerning vision:

We sought to reposition our company as one which would now meet a broader range of needs. We told our customers that we were in the packaging business, not the glass-container business. This was a relatively new thought for them. While our company was in plastics, at that time it was only in the portion-packaging niche and not in plastic containers.

We also told our customers about the strategic process we were following. We thought this would be helpful to them and to us. We described the fact gathering, the interviews we were conducting, the scope of the market as we saw it, the packaging possibilities, and our desire to get a much more complete understanding of their needs.

Beyond communicating to its major customers, Consumers Packaging sought to educate its stockholders and the broader business community about the shift to a Markets-Served vision. It carefully placed its strategic message in annual reports, in newspapers, and even in a specially produced videotape for television.

The headline that appeared on June 3, 1985, in the *Globe and Mail* (Toronto), just after the new strategy was born but prior to the name change, summed up what Consumers Packaging wanted to convey to key audiences. The headline read "Consumers Glass Puts Trust in Flexibility." As this and many other public-relations pieces went on to say, Consumers Packaging would meet a broader range of customer needs through business expansion, acquisition, and technological agreements in the plastics segments, while maintaining and preserving its glass operations. As the 1986 annual report concluded, strength in both segments and "our commitment to meeting the emerging market needs of our customers by expanding into high-technology packaging provide a solid base for future prosperity."

Discussing Strategy with Distributors or Suppliers

Dick Sosville of the Dow Chemical Company commented:

> We are finding how crucial it is to rethink traditional ways of dealing with distributors. Our strategy and theirs must be consistent and aimed at providing the best possible products and services to meet new and emerging needs of our target markets.
>
> What better way to do this than to share our strategy with each other? This identifies possible confusions, the most effective resource allocations, and required action plans for each other. We are committed to communicating our strategy to our distributors so that the ultimate end

user will get the best products at the best costs available in the marketplace.

A CONCLUDING WORD

The organizations we work with have a clear vision and have converted that vision to action. They have achieved the level of participation that is essential for reinforcing vision down through the organization so that action takes place. This represents the "aha's" we referred to in the first chapter.

But there are also "oh no's." As reality unfolds, there are always jagged edges of imperfection. Rarely is strategy implementation a perfect picture. The lessons learned from the strategic challenges that have confronted our organizations should make setting and implementing vision a little easier for all those committed to taking up the challenge. We discuss these lessons in the next chapter.

CHAPTER VII
The Lessons Learned

TODAY'S ORGANIZATION DEVELOPS AND ACHIEVES ITS VISION IN A WORLD where the old compass points of stability are no longer valid. No matter how insightful the vision or how skilled the implementation effort, the trek from strategy to operations is rarely predictable. Customer preferences may change in ways that your strategy never anticipated. Competitors may evade your best market intelligence. New technologies may appear that make your current products obsolete. Governments pass laws and take actions that unexpectedly derail you. New advocacy groups spring up to challenge the prevailing order. Countries that have slept for centuries now become powerful competitors. Companies are raided and dismembered, never mind your basic beliefs and strategy. Major champions of your organization's vision may move up or out. Key strategic capabilities may remain beyond your grasp. Current culture may refuse to bend to your organization's vision. The list is a long one, but here are the most common strategic challenges faced by the organizations we have worked with.

BASIC BELIEFS ARE BLOCKING VISION

In our experience, there is a tendency when formulating basic beliefs to settle, at least initially, for what "looks good" or "sounds right" rather than to achieve what reflects the true and deep-seated values of the organization. Those beliefs are few in number and are hard to articulate.

In one organization with which we worked—and it is not one of the organizations cited in this book—there was a lack of candor when it came to stating basic beliefs. At least, this was the judgment of one senior executive who participated in the strategic deliberations. We quote his comments anonymously:

> I don't think that we wrote down what our "real" basic beliefs were. We wrote down what was easy, not what we fundamentally felt and thought. We wrote about our belief in participation, but really believe in heavy-handed top management control. We said we believe in treating our employees fairly, yet our style is fairly punitive.
>
> I'm not saying we should publish these beliefs to the troops. However, we could have been honest among ourselves, got the beliefs out and asked, "Are these beliefs the right ones for the future?" The beliefs we identified did not get our strategic deliberations off to the right start.

Allan Nightingale of Courtaulds made a strong case for having the right beliefs as the foundation for strategic effort:

> Our initial strategy was less than totally successful because we didn't have a set of the proper basic beliefs up front of the effort. Every strategy is based on some obvious "home truths." In our case, these included the need for well-designed products that are produced to high-quality standards; getting the right cost/productivity base to ensure a competitive price; meeting international product standards; and, above all, finding customers who appreciate all that and are prepared to pay for it.
>
> In our next strategy go-around, we learned that these fundamentals had to be deeply felt at the value level, or the strategy would not succeed. They formed the basis of our operating culture.

As the Washington Mutual Financial Group moved from a Products-Offered to a Markets-Served direction, a basic belief slowed the transition. Al Doman explained:

Historically, the bank believed in the central control of its resources. Having tight control in a hierarchical structure was the way we thought the bank should operate.

However, as we moved in a Markets-Served direction, we felt the need to decentralize. But the old belief in centralization persisted. On the one hand, we were telling our managers, "We trust you; you must have increased responsibility and authority." On the other hand, we still wouldn't let them buy pencils without going through a big bureaucratic process. Until we came to terms with that belief, the total effectiveness of implementing our strategy was impaired.

Dennis Schwieger found that long-standing cultural values and beliefs can place subtle roadblocks in the way of successful strategy implementation. This can be particularly troublesome in a multinational setting:

I was at a meeting with some of the people who report directly to me. We were talking about Varity's tractor division strategy and the need for a worldwide structure in contrast to our historical geographical structure. I met a stone wall. The change was coming at them too forcefully. People in Europe like to discuss a problem and feel like part of the solution. We tried too hard to be a "good Yankee" and say, "Okay, guys, here's the objective; let's go get it." It's like an American football team, which sacrifices the individual interests of players to rush the halfback through the line. This is not done in Europe. Europeans play soccer. The attitude is "Screw the halfback. I'm going to be the hero."

The lesson learned is that outmoded or culturally jarring basic beliefs retard effective strategy implementation. They must be challenged and reevaluated for vision to move forward.

FAILURE TO GET STRATEGIC COMMITMENT

To our organizations, commitment is more than a human-relations gimmick. It is a prerequisite for strategic success.

One of the most impressive efforts to implement strategy was undertaken at Varity's tractor division in England. The top team carefully set a clear direction. It spent considerable time and effort communicating the vision and structuring participation down through the organization. Even with this thoughtful effort, one crucial ingredient was missing: Not all managers were committed to the new direction. Dennis Schwieger commented:

> At every level of the organization, we went to great lengths to implement the strategy. We had our entire organization involved. Each director was supposed to talk to everyone in his department about strategy and why we had chosen the Driving Force we did. We wanted everyone in the company, worldwide, to know where we were going and why we were headed in that direction. Beyond this, we had our people write personal, measurable performance objectives using our strategy as a reference point.
>
> But there was a flaw in our approach which all the effort could not solve. All the way up the line, a number of key people believed that our Driving Force should have been Markets Served rather than Products Offered. These people were not committed, and they failed to get involved in the implementation effort. Their attitude was "Let someone else worry about the strategy. I don't want to!"
>
> Consequently, central marketing was given the lion's share of responsibility for implementing the strategy. This attitude on the part of some really important players proved fatal to the full success of our strategic effort.

Abilene Christian University faced some unique difficulties in gaining commitment for the organization's vision. Bill Teague found that you just cannot decree common vision:

> Every faculty member at our university is really four separate people. First, he is an independent professional who is practicing his craft at a particular institution. His research and scholarly contribution are to benefit mankind, never mind the needs of the students or the direction

of our vision. Second, the faculty member is an employee, with all the needs, benefits, and perks of a professional employee. As an employee, resource constraints are hard for him to understand. Third, the faculty member is a boss or manager over the students. Fourth, the faculty member is a missionary.

To get even a modicum of strategic commitment, you constantly hammer at something that is larger and more important than the narrow attitudes of at least the first three people that make up each faculty member. This is not an easy task.

We must constantly remind the faculty of our vision: We are a different kind of school, we have a specific mission, we're eighty-one years deep into that mission, and that mission can be refined but not changed.

Chet Marks commented broadly on some of the issues around commitment that The Dow Chemical Company is guarding against:

During our application of the Kepner-Tregoe process, we identified several factors that guarantee self-destruction of strategic effort. One of the most obvious is the lack of consensus within any business team that is involved in our strategy. We'll know that we don't have consensus when bad-mouthing occurs. Someone says, "Damn, I spent three days attending a useless strategy meeting." By just saying that in the presence of a secretary, a manager is guaranteeing he will never get the strategy to work.

A second "self-destruct" factor is halfhearted participation. I have yet to see a team where we didn't eventually get everybody participating. But with some teams, I wondered whether or not we might have to change the composition.

A third factor is real poison: lack of senior management support. One of the reasons that the polyethylene and polystyrene work went so well was that the general manager participated in every strategy meeting with both businesses. He didn't dictate the strategy to the teams. But he was there, and he clearly demonstrated his interest.

The key lessons learned are simple but important: Without the continuing commitment of senior management to a uniform strategic direction, sub-businesses may go their own way. Do not assume your key people are easily committed to the organization's vision, particularly if they initially championed a different Driving Force. Test their commitment very carefully. Watch body language. Look for the reasons behind the reasons. If key people can be seen tossing the strategic "monkey" to staff executives or subordinates, your vision is probably in serious trouble. Every individual is a composite of different viewpoints, some of which may be in conflict. Vision must be the organizing principle that unites and drives those viewpoints.

MISSING REALITY TESTS

The Courtaulds Fabrics Group provides an example of an organization that set strategy but failed to do sufficient reality-testing. Its Products-Offered strategy produced a future-opportunities matrix with three broad product groups. While this made good conceptual sense, senior management just did not spend enough time reality-testing its conclusions before passing along the strategy to the three product groups for further refinement.

Noel Jervis explained why the consequences of this omission were severe:

> When we at group level were developing the future-opportunities matrix and setting future emphasis for the three product groups and their customers, we never assembled sufficient facts. We should have said, "We should be testing this." Or we should have said to the guys on the other side of the table, "That doesn't sound right—prove it is."
>
> I should have assumed more responsibility for improving the financial input to our strategic effort and said, "From a financial point of view, this seems wrong." I didn't do that. When the meetings were over, it was six o'clock, and I had to return to my office to do a day's work. We had

no resources. Maybe I should have fought for resources to provide stronger financial input.

Malcolm Vinnicombe shared Jervis's viewpoint at group level but saw a more positive outcome at unit level:

> One of the great weaknesses of the approach at Fabrics Group level was that most of the blessed numbers in the future-opportunities matrix were based on guesses. The necessary staff work was not done, and so we never verified what we were saying.
>
> However, all of that guesswork disappeared at unit level because we did it properly and got the staff work done. The matrix then became a much more powerful tool to kick the sacred cows and to show people which businesses we really needed to be in.

Noel Jervis also found a few positives in this situation:

> It was a question of horizon—the level of people's capability to think strategically and the very nature of the process. We weren't intellectually tested enough on some of the more narrow prejudices that the process brought out. That's not to say that the entire exercise wasn't very good in terms of helping our management to think strategically next time around, to verify that thinking, and to formulate plans in a better manner. From that point of view, what we did was extremely good.

The lesson here is: Allocate time and resources for reality-testing all strategic conclusions. For Kepner-Tregoe, this experience prompted a significant strengthening of independent reality-testing at each step in the process.

MISINTERPRETATIONS OF THE DRIVING FORCE

While the Driving Force is a fairly straightforward concept, recognizing the differences between Driving Forces and the true implications each has on an organization takes time and considerable thought. Bob Springmier of Dow Corning found that the subtle differences between Driving Forces belie the simplicity of the concept. This left room for misunderstanding:

> I was amazed at the opportunity for confusion about the intent of our Driving Force. When we presented our Driving Force to people who did not participate in the strategy formulation session, I was surprised at how often someone would say, "Oh, Technology is our Driving Force. Since I'm in the marketing department, and marketing is no longer important, I'd better get into R&D."
>
> Of course, I'm exaggerating to make the point. But we were concerned about misunderstanding of our strategic intent. So we were very careful about how we communicated the concept. We decided that only knowledgeable people should carry the communication burden.

At the OTC Group, Dale Johnson found that the Markets-Served Driving Force was taken to mean "Do it all for the customer."

> Some of our people were interpreting Markets Served as carte blanche for doing whatever had to be done to meet the customer's needs. For example, "Customer A" liked a specially designed piece of hydraulic equipment. The sales potential of this equipment was so small that it did not lead to other more profitable business. We proceeded anyway.
>
> Some of our people were using the Markets-Served Driving Force as an excuse to meet any need, even if that need required a product that fell outside of our product scope. Another difficulty was the feeling within operations, administration, and finance that sales and marketing were using Markets Served as a ploy to get whatever resources they wanted, whenever they wanted. This built up resistance to the strategy.
>
> We had to go back and enrich everyone's understanding of what a Markets-Served Driving Force was. We had to

come up with new, more specific criteria for reaching product and market conclusions.

Larry Reed discovered that it took a long time and a lot of patience for his team to understand Dow Corning's Technology Driving Force:

> When we revisited our strategy in 1981–82, our top management was still in the process of assimilating the meaning of our Technology Driving Force. Several years later, when we once again did a major review of the strategy, we had a more productive dialogue about Driving Force but still continued to deepen our understanding of the concept and the differentiation it implied for our business.
>
> Looking back, it was important to get management to understand all the nuances of the Driving-Force concept— what it means and doesn't mean and how it fits. That understanding took a lot of time.

Lee Shobe of Dow Chemical's plastics business commented on the confusion between a Products-Offered and a Markets-Served Driving Force:

> We have invested a tremendous amount of effort instilling in our people the need to change our marketing focus from "inside out" to "outside in." Unfortunately, the terminology of Products Offered versus Markets Served as alternative Driving Forces causes confusion. Many people equate Products Offered with "inside-out" marketing, and vice versa for Markets Served.
>
> We know this isn't true. The approach to marketing— inside out versus outside in—is really a "how-to" issue. It is independent of the choice of Driving Force. But the Driving Force terminology can present a communication difficulty we're working to overcome.

The lesson to be learned is that the Driving-Force concept is not a one-minute management solution. Neither should it become a full-time preoccupation. For most organizations, it takes a relatively short time to think through and agree upon a tentative Driving Force. But it takes far longer for the Driving Force to become ingrained in everyone's thinking so that it drives every facet of operations. It takes careful, critical, and challenging thought to understand the practical differences in various Driving Forces.

DEFICIENT STRATEGIC REWARD MECHANISMS

How do you build rewards for longer-term strategic accomplishment into a performance system which typically has been short term and operationally focused? The answer (only half facetiously) is—with great difficulty. Most of our organizations continue to struggle for solutions.

Shigeo Iiyama of Fuji Photo Film framed the difficulty:

> We have not really found a way to effectively separate strategic rewards from more immediate operational performance. Since there is little turnover, we can assess people over the long term. This enables us to give promotions for strategic performance. Short-term operational results are reflected in annual bonuses.
>
> We have been trying to balance both. But if we do not do a better job of finding ways to reward strategic performance, the probability of overlooking our strategic efforts will be great.

Frank Wobst knew that Huntington Bancshares was just beginning to resolve this issue:

> Right now, our reward system is based on an annual evaluation of performance. For example, incentives are paid if the parent company, Huntington Bancshares, earns a certain percentage on common equity during a twelve-month period. The higher the bank earnings during the fiscal year, the greater the incentive.

Incentives are not based on our strategic goals for return on equity over the next three to five years. We are not measuring performance over a longer time frame. We currently are exploring a way to build strategic performance objectives into our compensation system, at least for the top two tiers of management. It makes little sense to compensate people solely on the basis of the prior year's performance.

Merle Borchelt explained how he approaches strategic reward at the Central and South West Corporation:

I don't think you are really doing a thorough job of managing anybody until you build in a feedback system that tells you that your subordinates understand what you expect from them regarding the strategy. They also should know by what yardstick they are being measured, and what the rewards are for strategic accomplishment.

At senior levels, we've instituted restricted stock options, and we have begun to get the board to see the need to work out additional reward mechanisms to retain our top-level people. At middle-management levels, strategic reward mechanisms are another part of the human-resource planning process that we haven't been able to work out as effectively as we should. We don't know yet how their rewards can best fit in with the overall organization, given the strategic plan. But we're working on it.

Bob Morison provided insights into how Consumers Packaging is beginning to approach strategic reward:

For levels where we have an incentive system, we sit with our managers and determine the two or three operational objectives they must concentrate on during the next year. We have also added two or three objectives around the implementation of our strategy. So 50 percent of incentive award comes from standard divisional performance and 50 percent comes from strategic objectives.

Measuring performance against strategic objectives is not easy. Let me cite a specific. One of the underlying assumptions of our strategy involves projecting what the various provincial governments' positions will be on the issue of nonreturnable versus returnable bottles. We have to keep current on environmental matters.

I negotiate with my government-relations manager, and we agree that if he had ten contacts with appropriate elected officials in the ten provinces, this would be considered an outstanding strategic performance. Five contacts would be average. Fewer than that would be mediocre.

Under this reward system, the company or the manager's function could fail to meet operational performance targets. But that manager may still merit a bonus because of his performance against strategic objectives.

The lesson: If you want people to take aim and fire at the strategic target, they have to be motivated. Positive reinforcement for strategic behavior through—but not limited to—the compensation system is crucial. Precisely how to accomplish this is one of the toughest challenges of strategy implementation. It requires great thought on the part of organizations and the consultants that serve them. As we improve our ability to state, manage, and measure critical issues and key indicators of success, answering this challenge will become easier. Strategic reward mechanisms will not be perfect the first time around. Tolerance for failure, discussion, clear standards, and time are essential to resolving this issue.

STRATEGY IS DRIFTING

When the strategic process is first introduced to an organization, senior management may not have the discipline to keep the process moving along efficiently. Each major strategic conclusion needs time to be challenged or absorbed. But how much time? The answer must be part of an overall strategic timetable that moves smartly through each step of the strategy/

operations continuum, but allows time between steps for deep thinking and reflection. Otherwise, vision will drift.

Tom Tinmouth of Consumers Packaging expressed the difficulty this way:

> We first started working with Kepner-Tregoe in December of 1982, and now, more than seven years later, I'm not sure we've made the kind of strategic progress we should have. The reason is that there was too much of a time gap between strategic tasks. We didn't discipline ourselves to focus on a step in the process, complete the task in a timely fashion, analyze the results, work on the next step, and move ahead.
>
> We found ourselves reconnecting. There was such a time lapse between get-togethers that when we did get together, we had to go back for extensive review to jog our memories before we could move ahead.
>
> I assume some responsibility for this. I was part of the process and this problem. I recognize that, but still think we took too long to get where we are.

There are two lessons learned. First, organizations must develop and commit to an effective, timely schedule upon which to proceed in setting and implementing vision. Second, our lesson as consultants is this: Keep a proper balance between time to digest and time to move forward.

STRATEGY AND PLANNING—THE ENDS DON'T MEET

Motohiro Takaya of the Kawasaki Steel Corporation discussed when bottom-up planning and top-down vision do not meet:

> For the past several years, we focused on reducing costs. This effort has been successful, but it has reached its limit. There is only so far you can go, and, besides, cost-reduction efforts, at least in Japan, tend to be a bottom-up activity.

What we have right now is very low cost on a product that is reaching the end of its life cycle. We need to focus our bottom-up planning and activity on the implications of our Driving Force. Should we even be in this product, given our Driving Force? Can this product be modified to extend its life? We must bring our strategic and operational planning together.

Ben Goodman observed that Consumers Packaging has not successfully integrated its new corporate Markets-Served direction into the glass division, the company's largest profit center:

In the glass-container profit center, I don't see any dramatic changes in the way we approach planning compared with what we did three or four years ago. There have been some modest changes, but nothing really significant in terms of integrating planning with the new corporate strategy. This cannot continue.

In fact, it is not continuing. Consumers Packaging is now rapidly building strategy into the plans of both the glass and plastics divisions.

The lesson learned: If what you want to be is not integrated with your operating plans, then at best the two might meet informally. This is a high-risk dice toss that typically leads to strategy and planning veering off in different directions. This situation demands top management's most urgent attention.

STRATEGIC PARTICIPATION TO A FAULT

While there are many benefits of broad strategic participation, in some instances the degree of participation should be more deeply evaluated.

Victor Rice of Varity put this point in tight perspective:

I'm not quite sure how much involvement middle managers should have. Very few middle managers really have sufficient power to actually implement strategy. Middle managers also tend to be specialists and really do not have to know the entire vision.

Participation usually implies involvement, but not always. At Central and South West Corporation, Durwood Chalker wanted managers from the operating businesses to participate in the effort to communicate corporate strategy. He aimed not to get broad involvement in the overall strategy but to guide and motivate these managers to set their own strategy.

> Our overall holding-company strategy did not require direct involvement or action on the part of the four operating electric utilities. But we wanted to share the overall strategy and demonstrate the necessity of having each operating utility maintain its own strategy and effective operations. This would increase the holding company's probability of achieving its strategy.

Larry Reed of Dow Corning struck the proper balance between "need to know" and "nice to know":

> People down the line do not have to know all the details about Dow Corning's strategy. Our objectives were to ensure that people knew we used a valid strategic process and to ensure that they clearly understood what the implications were for their operation.

The lesson here is: Gear participation to need. Knowing more than you need to know may be nice, but not necessary—and it can get in the way.

OUR STRATEGY FACILITATORS NEED HELP

For more complex organizations, we trained in-house strategy facilitators to help manage the detailed implementation of the process. This worked reasonably well, but the comments that follow point to the difficulties.

Peter Aubusson of the Courtaulds Fabrics Group discussed some of his frustrations in the role of strategy facilitator:

> Chris Pickup [the other strategy facilitator in the Fabrics Group] and I received thorough training in the strategy process. We were technically up to speed. But the thing you cannot give someone in our situation is the breadth of consulting experience that an outside resource possesses. An experienced consultant can pull out the appropriate examples, quickly spot misinterpretations, and challenge superficial thinking. He has faced all the tough issues before.
>
> Another difficulty was in the ambiguity of our role. Should we lead or follow? Should we make value judgments during the discussions or remain neutral?
>
> A third difficulty stemmed from the fact that we were in-house consultants. Since we have to continue to work with everyone after the strategy sessions are done, it's tough to really challenge someone. You can't say, "That's a lot of bull."

Noel Jervis of the Courtaulds Fabrics Group pointed to another difficulty with in-house strategy facilitators:

> After the strategy exercise was initially concluded, the facilitators returned to their full-time jobs. For example, Peter Aubusson was head of market research for fabrics. One year later, he became head of market research for the total textile group. This new assignment took 100 percent of his time.
>
> In addition, our other facilitator, Chris Pickup, became involved in running a velvet-manufacturing company we acquired. Both our facilitators were lost, and that crippled implementation.

Dennis Schwieger of Varity's tractor division faced almost the reverse difficulty. He found himself carrying the strategic load, and this presented difficulties of its own:

We had to get the strategic message across to five hundred middle managers in four different languages. I was one of the facilitators who was trained to accomplish the task.

Given my role in marketing and planning, my office became the central seat or treasure box for the division's strategy. That was a mistake. I began doing more than anyone else to implement the strategy. It became easy for the other directors to have me carry their implementation burden. For example, when I ran an implementation session for middle managers, some of the directors would say to me, "Listen, I don't have the time. Could my people join your session?"

This led to difficulty. When middle managers made commitments during the sessions, they would write them down and then send them to their director. Nothing happened. The directors often sat back and said, "Wait a minute. This commitment was made to Dennis, but it wasn't made to me."

Chet Marks of Dow Chemical suggested that all these difficulties need resolution, given the critical role of facilitators:

We realize how important it is to have ongoing facilitators to ensure that our strategy is implemented. We have stressed the need to implement our strategic vision all the way to the individual employee on the shop floor and in the field sales office. But we've underestimated the time needed to provide continuing support.

While we continue to believe in the importance of an outside consultant to help formulate strategy and build the initial bridges to implementation, we have learned that the implementation process needs internal facilitators.

The lessons learned: First, the roles of both the internal facilitators and outside consultants must be carefully defined so both are used effectively. Those aspects of the process requiring broad consulting experience should be left to the external consultants. Second, the role of the internal facilitator must be ongoing, with sufficient time allocated to meet the demands of that role. Third, neither internal nor external facilitators can assume the strategic responsibility that rightfully belongs to management. In that case, the facilitator will be the only one committed. Finally, outside consultants must work diligently with their client organizations to establish this role effectively.

MISALIGNED INFORMATION SYSTEMS

. . . Due to a Change in Driving Force

STAN HANNAFORD: If you looked at our financial reporting system, you would think Consumers Packaging had remained Products Offered or Low-Cost Production Capability driven, as opposed to Markets Served driven.

We have a strict product-line reporting system that is detailed and goes right down to an analysis of production variances. However, we are weak in capturing financial and marketing data and reporting them on a market-segment basis that cuts across glass-and-plastics divisional lines. To begin collecting those kinds of data, we must go back to the general ledger and the chart of accounts.

BILL CAMPBELL: Stan's financial group is responding with all the planning tools to make the new strategic information system happen. We still have a ways to go. We can't supply information that is organized around customer groups. For example, we need answers tó questions like "How much business are we currently doing in food at home or in wines and spirits? Is it profitable?"

Consumers Packaging is probably five years away from having an integrated information system that crosses divisions. It seems a heck of a long way away. But it takes time to get there.

. . . Due to a Change in Segmentation

AARON JONES: The weakness in the Products-Offered strategy at Varity's tractor division, and in our attempt to segment by end user rather than by geography, was the lack of information. We always retrieved information by country and not by how products were used, such as for narrow- or wide-row grain farming, vineyards, or orchards.

The information just wasn't there. No matter how rough, we must have information by product end user on a worldwide basis for our Products-Offered approach to succeed. If we're really going after the narrow-row grain, vineyard, or orchard farmer on a worldwide basis, we simply must get the relevant industry information.

... Due to the Technical Specialist

DICK JOHNSON: We must overcome the tendency in Dow Chemical's U.S. Plastics Group to drive the management information systems' [MIS] plans and resource expenditures primarily from the exciting new technological developments in the MIS field. We need to be on the leading edge but use the technologies that best support the information requirements of our business strategies and plans.

This means a major communications effort. Our MIS technologists must learn about the information needs of the business strategy. Then they must be able to show business strategy managers how the new and emerging MIS technologies can meet their information needs.

The lesson learned is that even though we are in an information revolution, executives still tend to underestimate the difficulty of having the appropriate information systems to support their vision. Those responsible for strategy and those providing information must get together early. If the vision calls for new kinds of information to measure and monitor strategic effectiveness, then find ways to retrieve that information, or be prepared to guess about results.

TASK-FORCE FADE-OUT

Strategic task forces are used with increasing frequency to stimulate creativity and provide motivation and commitment for change. We have presented many examples of the use of task forces. But without careful thought and management, a task force may not live up to its promise. The task-force experience at Consumers Packaging is a case in point.

Tom Tinmouth began the story:

> In retrospect, one of the lessons we learned with the strategic task forces is the need to take a *hands-off* approach.
>
> One fine day, a senior executive discovered that he was unhappy with what he heard coming from one of the task forces. He charged into the meeting room and proceeded to unload on the members of the group. That subverted the effort.
>
> Obviously, we must monitor the work of task forces. If we are concerned about the direction they are taking, then we ought to talk about the problem. Trying to dictate to a task force kills the effort.

Craig Blizzard continued:

> The work of our task force was exciting. At times, however, it was a bit overwhelming. We had to meet our everyday responsibilities and simultaneously devote a significant amount of time, attention, and resources to the strategy project. It was a challenge to properly handle both responsibilities.

Frank Fabian summarized:

> One of the responsibilities of our task force was to examine new technologies to satisfy new needs. But at the same time we were making this assessment, senior management signed several new technology-licensing agreements without our knowledge or input. While our work supported what was done, we were surprised at being usurped. This was a real downer.
>
> The task force worked for about a year, and we did make some recommendations. Toward the end, meetings

of the team were continually delayed or postponed. Managers rarely talked about their assignment on the task force anymore.

Then meetings just stopped happening altogether. Nobody ever figured out why. It really would have been helpful and motivating to bring all our work to a final conclusion.

The lesson: Strategic involvement through task forces requires top management to first manage its own decision-making behavior. It must carefully delineate responsibility to avoid preempting the prerogatives entrusted to task-force participants. In addition, strategic task forces have a life cycle all their own. Each phase of that life cycle, from initially establishing the charter to the formal conclusion, must be managed skillfully.

STRATEGIC CONTINUITY, MANAGERIAL DISCONTINUITY

Ideally, managers who set strategy will stay in place until that strategy is well into implementation. But this is not always possible. Good people are in great demand. Some stay with their current organization but get promoted. Others move out or retire. Maintaining strategic continuity in the face of turnover is a tough challenge.

At Varity Corporation, Peter Barton learned that managers who struggled together to formulate and implement strategy have a unique, personal relationship with the vision. This is not easy to replicate:

> We've got a tightly knit management group that went up the mountain and set strategy in a series of intense, three-day sessions. We emerged from the experience feeling even more of a team, with a real consensus about where we wanted to go.
>
> Then, over time, management changes occurred. One or two people left, and new executives joined the team.

Whenever this occurs, whether at divisional or corporate level, there's a built-in resistance on the part of a new member to take at face value what everyone else in the group internalized long ago. It is very difficult to bring a new man on and make him feel part of the strategy without boring everyone else in the process.

Tom Tinmouth of Consumers Packaging provided an answer to Barton's "new-man-on-the-block" difficulty:

The only way you can pass the torch to an incoming executive is by sitting down with him. You must take time for in-depth discussions of the strategic process, for getting him to understand the strategy and why it makes sense.

Jim Bacon, who heads up our plastics operation, is a good example. He came into the company less than two years ago. Jim got exposed to our strategy many years after it was already put in place. He didn't have the opportunity to understand the process as the rest of us did, and he didn't understand our strategy to the extent we did. At first, he couldn't visualize how our strategic thinking could help in his operations. He needed that time.

Ron Lehrer, who runs the packaging industry for Dow Chemical's plastic businesses, commented on the problem of continuity and provided at least a partial solution:

We are always changing jobs around here. Even though these changes represent the strength of our matrix structure, they pose a problem for making sure our strategies are implemented. But often the key people involved in setting the strategy for a specific business are off on another assignment when we get to the issues of implementation.

Having a common strategic process helps to offset the difficulty. It provides a common language and methodology. A new person in a specific business can catch up quickly with the thinking that has gone on prior to his involvement. He can integrate his own thinking into the business team without destroying the commitment and momentum that have already been achieved.

Perhaps the surest, but most difficult to achieve, solution to the problem of strategic continuity belongs to Jack Snedeker:

> I've been in my current position for more than six years. That's a long time at Dow Corning, but such tenure is critical to implementing strategy. To be meaningful, strategy must be a four- to five-year process, and it's a very personal thing.
>
> If someone took over from me when the strategy was only half implemented, the chances are he would move in some new direction. It would be fairly easy to do. Since I have been working on our strategy for more than five years, a new person would need to work mighty hard to change things. The strategy is now fully operational.

Lessons learned: Try not to rock the management boat until strategy has become integrated with operations. If a key manager leaves, a strategic void has been created. Recognize that his replacement, even though he may have been part of the strategic process, has his own ideas and style. He must make his own imprint. He may keep the same strategy but frame it his way. Take special care to prepare this incoming manager. A sound process, clear vision, and a common language are good guides to resolving a void in continuity.

A CONCLUDING WORD

When all the process insights and points about technique have been made, vision remains primarily a judgment call. Vision deals with future uncertainty. It addresses how an organization can survive and grow, given the ability of its employees to think incisively about the future and to harness resources accordingly.

At the most basic level, vision entails coming to grips with two conceptual challenges. First, there is a need to focus the strategic choices confronting an organization. The Driving Force is a powerful concept to meet this challenge.

Second, there is a need to translate vision into future product, market, and capability plans. The future opportunities matrix is a powerful guide.

As vision moves along the strategy/operations continuum and down through the organization, it takes broad and effective participation to make it come to life. Through it all, vision must be kept clear, specific, and simple—simple enough to put in the heads, hearts, and hands of the people who make an organization what it is and what it will become.

Frank Fabian of Consumers Packaging said in a very personal way what we hope every middle manager, individual contributor, and employee feels about strategic decision making in his organization:

> Having worked in the glass division for twelve years, I had a fairly narrow focus on what life was really all about at Consumers Packaging. We really didn't know what was going on at the corporate office regarding the longer-term viability of the corporation. The strategic effort and the actions that have been taken indicate that someone in the company is serious about vision. It's gratifying to see something positive happening and to know how much attention senior management is paying to our future. Input continues to be solicited from those in the operating groups who have close customer contact and good technical or production knowledge. This is motivating, as it assures us of the reality of senior management's thinking.
>
> I feel a lot better about our direction, especially in talking with our customers. They feel we are doing the right things and that our actions fit with their plans.
>
> The last three years have been extremely beneficial in getting our staff attuned to the vision and in keeping a high profile with our customer base.

Jack Ludington of Dow Corning provided a fitting summation when we asked him what he felt was the most important strategic legacy a CEO could leave his company:

> The key is to leave behind not just one person but a cadre of competent people with the talent to run the company. These people may not always agree with one another, or they may do things differently. But what unites them is a common vision about where the organization is headed.
>
> This cadre of people must have the ability to change direction when change is needed. But they must proceed with thoughtful deliberation. They must realize that all of us are not fully masters of our own fate. We are living in a world that is changing dramatically, be it market, product, capability, or political or social change.
>
> The best legacy is to leave an organization with people who are gifted enough to set a clear strategic direction, committed enough to bring it about, and courageous enough to admit that the vision may have to be modified or changed with the passage of time.

All the rest is discipline, detail, and dedicated strategic effort.

APPENDIX A

Organization Profiles and Individuals Interviewed

THE FOLLOWING ARE BRIEF PROFILES OF EACH ORGANIZATION FEATURED IN this book. We have also listed the names of all the individual members of these organizations whom we interviewed, along with their titles at the time of the interviews.

Abilene Christian University, located in Abilene, Texas, is the fourth-largest private university in the Southwest and the largest university affiliated with the Church of Christ. Total enrollment is approximately 4,300 students.

The university consists of five colleges, a graduate school, and a nursing school. The colleges are the College of Liberal and Fine Arts, College of Biblical Studies, College of Natural and Applied Sciences, College of Professional Studies, and College of Business Administration.

The university employs approximately 235 faculty members, and more than 70 percent hold doctorates or the equivalent. Baccalaureate degrees are offered in eighty-six fields, master's degrees in forty-four fields, and a Doctor of Ministry degree is also offered.

Individuals Interviewed:

- Carl Brecheen
  Professor of Bible

- Ian Fair
  Dean, College of Bible Studies

- C. G. Gray
  Vice-President for Academic Affairs

- Bill J. Humble
  Director, Center for Restorations

- Clinton E. Hurley
  Dean of Academic Support

- Gary McCaleb
  Vice-President and Dean of Campus Life

- William J. Teague
  President

- Joyce Whitefield
  Director, University Development Services

Central and South West Corporation, with headquarters in Dallas, Texas, is a public utility holding company with four electric subsidiary companies. These four subsidiary companies provide electricity to 4,150,000 people in an area covering 152,000 square miles. Central Power and Light operates in south Texas. Public Service Company of Oklahoma operates in eastern and southeastern Oklahoma. Southwestern Electric Power Company operates in northwestern Louisiana, northeastern Texas, and western Arkansas. West Texas Utilities Company operates in central and west Texas. In addition, Central and South West owns six other subsidiaries, four of which are diversification ventures. Central and South West employs 8,894 people and had operating revenues for 1987 of some $2.4 billion.

Individuals Interviewed:

- Merle Borchelt
  Vice-President

- Durwood Chalker
  Chairman and Chief Executive Officer

- John E. Taulbee
  Executive Vice-President and Chief Financial Officer

Consumers Packaging, Inc. (formerly Consumers Glass, Inc.), is a leading Canadian producer of a high-quality glass containers and plastics packaging, serving the food, fast-food, beverage, brewery, distilling, wines, cosmetic and toiletries, and pharmaceutical industries. The company operates fourteen manufacturing plants in North America—twelve in Canada and two in the United States. Consumers Packaging is headquartered in Toronto, Canada. Sales volume for 1987 was some $324 million.

Individuals Interviewed:

- D. Craig Blizzard
  Director of Marketing and Sales for Portion Packaging

- William S. Campbell
  Executive Vice-President, Corporate Marketing and Development

- Frank J. Fabian
  Director of Sales, New Business Development

- Lieven Gevaert
  Manager, Quality and Service

- Benjamin Goodman
  Director of Distribution, Container and Closure Products

- Zohir Handy
  Director, Corporate Marketing

- S. W. Hannaford
  Vice-President, Finance and Administration

- Gerald Joseph Kavanagh
  Vice-President and General Manager, Container and Closure Products

- Duncan Stewart Kennedy
  Vice-President, New Business Development

- R. D. Morison
  President and Chief Executive Officer

- Thomas A. Tinmouth
  Executive Vice-President and Chief Operating Officer

Courtaulds Fabrics Group is part of the Textiles Group, a division of Courtaulds, PLC. The company is headquartered in London, England, and was founded in 1816 to weave silk. Having successfully pioneered man-made fibers, Courtaulds has used its technological skills and market positions to extend its activities across a wide range of industries around the world. The group's chemical and industrial products are man-made fibers, advanced materials, fine chemicals, wood pulp, coatings, and packaging materials. It also is a major supplier, directly and indirectly, of textiles and clothing to consumer markets. Courtaulds, PLC, employs 65,000 people and has sales of some $2.3 billion. The Fabrics Group is a major weaver of fabrics for apparel, home furnishings, and industrial applications.

Individuals Interviewed:

- Peter Aubusson
  Market Analysis Manager, Textiles Group

- John Billing
  Director, Management Services, Textiles Group

- James Connor
  Chief Executive, Home Furnishings Group

- Fredrick Dixon
  Chief Executive, Derby-Nyla

- Noel Jervis
  Financial Director, Textiles Group

- J. A. Nightingale
  Chairman, Textiles Group

- John P. Stevenson
  Chief Executive, Weft Knitting

- John Hugh Sturgess
  Director of Marketing, Textiles Group

- David G. Suddens
  Chairman, Apparel Fabrics Division

- Malcolm Vinnicombe
  Chief Executive, Finishing and Converting Division

- Geoffrey Woods
  Chief Executive, Fabric Weaving

The Dow Chemical Company is a global producer of basic and specialty chemicals, plastics, and pharmaceutical and agricultural products, with international headquarters in Midland, Michigan. Worldwide sales in 1987 totaled some $13.5 billion, divided approximately equally between the United States and the rest of the world.

Individuals Interviewed:

- Kurt Fleig
  Manager of Pharmaceuticals, Latin American Area, Merrell Dow Pharmaceuticals, Inc.

- Carlos Gonzales
  Specialty Products Department Manager, Latin American Area

- Kenneth D. Harman
  Business Director, Styrene Polymers, U.S. Area Plastics Group

- J. Richard Johnson
  Director of Business Resources, U.S. Area Plastics Group

- Ronald G. Lehrer
  Vice-President, Packaging Industry, U.S. Area Plastics Group

- C. D. (Chet) Marks
  Director, Planning and New Venture Development, U.S. Area Plastics Group

- M. Kenneth Mitchell
  Business Director, Polyethylene, U.S. Area Plastics Group

- Lee A. Shobe
  Vice-President, Sales and Marketing, U.S. Area Plastics Group

- Richard E. Sosville
  Marketing Director, Durables Industry, U.S. Area Plastics Group

Dow Corning Corporation is a 50/50 joint venture of Corning Glass Works and The Dow Chemical Company. The company's principal business is to develop, manufacture, and market silicones, related specialty chemical materials, polycrystalline silicon, and certain specialty health-care products. The company's products serve virtually all major industries, including transportation, communications, electrical/electronics, construction, aerospace, government, personal care, and health care.

Dow Corning is a high-technology company which invests 7 to 8 percent of its annual sales in research. The company is a multinational enterprise with roughly one-half of its business outside the United States. Sales in 1987 were approximately $1.3 billion. Dow Corning is headquartered in Midland, Michigan.

Individuals Interviewed:

- J. Kermit Campbell
  Vice-President, Personnel, Communications and Public Affairs

- John S. Ludington
  Chairman and Chief Executive Officer

- Lawrence A. Reed
  President and Chief Operating Officer

- John P. Snedeker
  Vice-President and General Manager, Elastomers and Engineering Industries Business

- Robert S. Springmier
  Director, Corporate Planning

- Edward Steinhoff
  Chief Financial Officer

- Donald R. Weyenberg
  Vice-President, Research and Development

The Federal Reserve Bank of Cleveland is one of twelve regional reserve banks in the United States, which, together with the Board of Governors in Washington, D.C., make up the nation's central bank. The Federal Reserve System is responsible for formulating and implementing U.S. monetary policy, supervising banks and bank holding companies, and providing financial services to depository institutions and the federal government.

The Federal Reserve System was created in 1913. The Federal Reserve Bank of Cleveland, its two branches in Cincinnati and Pittsburgh, and its Regional Check Processing Center in Columbus serve the Fourth Federal Reserve District. The Fourth District includes Ohio, western Pennsylvania, the northern panhandle of West Virginia, and eastern Kentucky.

Individuals Interviewed:

- William H. Hendricks
  First Vice-President

- Karen Horn
  President

- Edward E. Richardson
  Vice-President, Services Management

- Robert F. Ware
  Senior Vice-President

Fuji Photo Film Company, Ltd., designs, manufactures, and markets worldwide a wide range of consumer photographic, magnetic, and commercial products. Fuji Film is the largest manufacturer in Japan of photographic film and photographic paper. In addition to its extensive overseas sales distribution and processing network, Fuji Film also has overseas manufacturing facilities in the Netherlands and West Germany. Overseas sales account for some 35 percent of the company's total net sales. Total revenues are about $5.2 billion. Fuji Film employs approximately 11,000 people and has headquarters in Tokyo.

Individuals Interviewed:

- Shigeo Iiyama
  Manager, Personnel Department

- Keigo Kosaka
  Senior Staff, Personnel Department

Gund Investment Corporation (GIC) is a privately held investment company in Princeton, New Jersey, whose principal owner, president, and chief executive officer is Gordon Gund. GIC is a corporate service organization providing a wide range of investment and professional management services to its investment activities. Services provided by GIC include strategic planning, management oversight and assistance with banking relationships, legal requirements, financial analysis, tax planning, accounting, human resources, and administration.

Individuals Interviewed:

- Gordon Gund
  Chairman and President

Huntington Bancshares, Inc., is a regional bank holding company headquartered in Columbus, Ohio. The company's banking, trust, investment and mortgage banking, and other subsidiaries operate 236 offices located in Ohio, Michigan, Kentucky, Indiana, Florida, Pennsylvania, Virginia, Maryland, and Illinois. Total bank assets are more than $9 billion, and the company employs 5,500 people.

Individuals Interviewed:

- T. Carl Alderman
  President and Chief Operating Officer, Huntington National Bank

- Robert Lentz
  Senior Vice-President

- Zuheir Sofia
  President and Chief Operating Officer

- Frank Wobst
  Chairman and Chief Executive Officer

The J. M. Smucker Company was founded in 1897. It manufactures and markets food products, including preserves, jams, jellies, orange marmalade, ice cream toppings, fruit butters, low-calorie preserves and jellies, fruit and fruit products, peanut butter, and industrial fruit products such as bakery fillings and dairy fillings, juice beverages, ketchup, and mustard. "Smucker's" has approximately 1,500 employees and is located in Orrville, Ohio. Sales volume is approximately $350 million.

Individuals Interviewed:

- William P. Boyle, Jr.
  Senior Vice-President, Marketing, and President International

- Robert Ellis
  Director, Human Resources

- Alan McFalls
  Vice-President, Corporate Development

- John D. Milliken
  Vice-President, Logistics

- Robert R. Morrison
  Vice-President, Operations

- Paul H. Smucker
  Chairman of the Executive Committee and Chief Executive Officer

- Richard Kim Smucker
  President

- Timothy Paul Smucker
  Chairman

Kawasaki Steel Corporation is the seventh-largest steel firm in the free world, with a dominant position in flat-rolled, high-quality steel products such as steel sheets for the automotive market. Kawasaki Steel also has diversified into high-growth, non-steel areas such as electronics and urban development. Four steel-making plants operate in Japan. There are affiliated operations in Brazil, the Philippines, and the United States. The company employs approximately 22,500 people, generates some $6.8 billion in revenue, and is headquartered in Tokyo.

Individuals Interviewed:

- Motohiro Takaya
  Staff Manager, Steel Business Planning Division, Technology and Production Planning Department

NISSAY (formerly Nippon Life Insurance Company) is the largest life insurance company in the world in total assets and insurance income, with total assets totaling some $134 billion. NISSAY's holdings in real estate rank it as one of the top real estate companies in Japan. Headquartered in Osaka and Tokyo, it has 121 branches nationwide that work with 1,991 sub-branches to assist some 72,000 sales representatives. The company recently has expanded business internationally. It has established an international monetary department and has multiplied the number of foreign subsidiaries. NISSAY employs 91,000 people.

Individuals Interviewed:

- Koji Hayashi
  General Manager, Educational Department

- Kenichi Kinoshita
  Supervisory Manager, Educational Department

- Masaaki Shibamoto
  Deputy General Manager, Educational Department

Oki Electric Industry Company, Ltd., is 110 years old and is one of the major electronics makers in Japan. Its main products are in the communication-systems area. It manufactures electronic switching systems, data-processing systems, applied electronic systems, and related equipment. The company operates eight plants in Japan and eleven subsidiaries overseas. Oki Electric Industry Company employs some 14,000 people and generates a revenue of approximately $3 billion. The company's main office is located in Tokyo.

Individuals Interviewed:

- Hiroshi Inoue
  General Manager, Megabit DRAM R&D Department, Electronic Devices Group

- Kiyoshi Yanagawa
  Manager, Education Section, Administration Division, Electronic Devices Group

- Toshiki Yokokawa
  General Manager, Electronic Components Division, Electronic Devices Group

- Mitsuo Yoshida
  General Manager, Quality Reliability Division

The **OTC Group** (formerly the Owatonna Tool Company) has five divisions that manufacture and market automotive specialized service tools and equipment, electronic diagnostic equipment, window and door hardware, and hydraulic rams and pumps for industrial applications. OTC is a unit of SPX Corporation, a Fortune 500 company which manufactures and distributes precision automotive parts and components, specialized service tools and equipment, and industrial products to both domestic and international markets. The OTC Group is headquartered in Owatonna, Minnesota.

Individuals Interviewed:

- Roger Ahrens
  Production Inventory Control Manager

- Charles Hough, Jr.
  Vice-President, Sales and Marketing

- R. W. Kaplan
  Chairman of the Board

- Dale Johnson
  President

- Erwin D. Lowell
  Manager, Electronics Plant

- James A. Schultz
  Hydraulics Plant Manager

- Larry Stordahl
  Vice-President, Operations

- John Tacheny
  Director, Sales and Product Development, Truth Division

R. P. Foundation Fighting Blindness was founded in 1971. It is a national eye-research foundation dedicated to finding a cure for degenerative retinal diseases such as retinitis pigmentosa (RP), Usher's syndrome (deafness and RP), and macular degeneration, which affect approximately 400,000 Americans and, as a group, are the leading causes of blindness and deaf-blindness in the United States. The Baltimore-based foundation supports basic and clinical research at more than thirty prominent institutions in the United States and foreign countries, and serves as a worldwide source of information for RP specialists, professionals, and affected families. The foundation has sixty affiliates in the United States and nineteen in foreign countries, with 35,000 volunteers.

Individuals Interviewed:

- Gordon Gund
  Chairman

Showa Denko K.K. is the parent company of the Showa Denko group of sixty companies. The group's business activities span every aspect of synthetic chemicals, from chemical raw materials to finished chemicals such as olefins, plastics, organic chemicals, inorganic chemicals, biochemicals, carbons, ceramics, and others. Recently, the company has undertaken new ventures in data processing and financial services. Showa Denko employs about 5,000 people, has a revenue of approximately $3.2 billion, and is headquartered in Tokyo.

Individuals Interviewed:

- Yoshihiro Hirose
  Manager, Sales Department, Plastics Division

Varity Corporation (formerly Massey-Ferguson, Ltd.) is a management holding company with headquarters in Toronto, Canada. Its operating businesses design, manufacture, and distribute farm and industrial machinery, diesel engines, and automotive and hydraulic components internationally. Some of these companies are market leaders, such as Massey-Ferguson, the Western world's largest producer of tractors; Perkins Engines, the world's largest supplier of diesel engines to original-equipment manufacturers; and Dayton-Walther, a leading supplier of wheel-end components to North American manufacturers of trucks and trailers. Varity's sales volume is approximately $2.3 billion.

Individuals Interviewed:

- Peter N. Barton
  Vice-President, Business Development

- James M. Felker
  Senior Vice-President, Development

- Aaron Jones
  Director of Finance and Administration,
  Massey-Ferguson

- Victor Albert Rice
  Chairman and Chief Executive Officer

- Wilfried Sander
  General Manager, Parts, Massey-Ferguson

- Dennis E. Schwieger
  Director of Projects, Massey-Ferguson

Washington Mutual Financial Group (formerly the Washington Mutual Savings Bank), with headquarters in Seattle, Washington, consists of the Washington Mutual Savings Bank and its subsidiaries. The state-chartered stock savings bank attracts deposits from the general public and makes residential, commercial real estate, and consumer loans. Its subsidiaries include a federal savings bank and companies providing full-service securities brokerage, mutual-fund management, financial counseling, retirement-plan consulting and administration, and insurance and travel-agency services. The bank and its subsidiaries have consolidated assets of $6.1 billion.

Individuals Interviewed:

- Alan J. Doman
  Senior Vice-President

- Kerry K. Killinger
  Senior Executive Vice-President

- William Longbrake
  Senior Executive Vice-President

- Louis Pepper
  Chairman, Chief Executive Officer, and President

APPENDIX B
Driving-Force Descriptions

In addition to the Products-Offered, Markets-Served, and Return/Profit Driving Forces discussed in Chapter 2, our research suggests that there are five remaining Driving Forces that can determine the nature and direction of an organization.* A description of each of these follows, along with examples of well-known companies that exemplify each Driving Force. Since we have not set the strategy of any of the organizations we cite, we are taking an educated guess. See if you agree with the examples.

TECHNOLOGY

An organization pursuing a Technology Driving Force builds its strategic vision around a body of knowledge, or a set of technological capabilities. It has the people and the physical

---

* In *Top Management Strategy*, "Method of Sale" and "Method of Distribution" were described as separate Driving Forces. Time and experience have taught us to combine them as one driving force—Method of Distribution/Sale "Size/Growth" was also a source of Driving Force. We have also learned that size/growth is a strategic consideration for all Driving Forces but is not a source in itself. If size/growth expectations or requirements are sufficiently high compared with current strategic expectations, they may force a change in Driving Force. Also, Production Capability has been divided into two more descriptive sources for Driving Force—Low-Cost Production Capability and Operations Capability.

resources to develop this basic technology and to apply it in innovative ways in order to satisfy existing, emerging, or completely new needs.

The Technology organization's competitive advantage rests in the unique quality or quantity of this technological expertise and the ability to generate a wide range of applications of this technology. It will strive to stay at the forefront of its chosen technology, changing the boundaries under which it operates as the technology advances. It will be considered a leader in its chosen field.

The organization with a Technology Driving Force may choose to retain control over its technological capability by producing products or services emanating from the technology base. However, some Technology-driven organizations keep their focus on the technology base, licensing or joint-venturing aspects or applications of the technology to others for product development and production.

The business priorities of a Technology organization will depend on the nature of the technological capability and will generally follow this pattern:

1. Offer existing product applications of its technology to existing customer groups.

2. Offer existing product applications of its technology to new customer groups or new product applications to current customer groups.

3. Provide new applications of its technology to new customer groups.

   Example: Minnesota Mining and Manufacturing Company

LOW-COST PRODUCTION CAPABILITY

An organization pursuing a Low-Cost Production Capability Driving Force has a set of production capabilities able to produce products or services at the lowest cost relative to competitive offerings. This type of organization will maintain and increase its cost advantage over its competitors through advanced process technology and cost-conscious management of its production. It will use its knowledge of advances in process technology or production methods to stay ahead of competitors and to avoid obsolescence of its production capabilities.

Because of the nature of the product capabilities, economies of scale are important. The organization guided by Low-Cost Production Capability will produce standard products consistent with its capabilities, maintaining steady and high production levels or ensuring ready availability of large volumes. Products will be competitive in their features and benefits, but differentiated by their low price.

This type of organization will target markets or customer groups where price is the principal buying motive and where desired quantities match its production capabilities. The organization may also produce for others the same products it produces for itself.

The business priorities of a Low-Cost Production Capability organization generally follow this pattern:

1. Increase its penetration in current markets with its current or modified products.

2. Offer these products to new target markets.

   Example: International Paper Company

OPERATIONS CAPABILITY

An organization pursuing an Operations Capability Driving Force has a set of capabilities—physical, human, and technical—which, used in a variety of combinations, produces a wide range of products or services. The organization's competitive advantage stems from these capabilities and the ability to use them flexibly, allocating the appropriate mix of capabilities to deliver specific products or services. This organization will seek maximum use of its capabilities by controlling capacity in response to the demand or seeking innovative ways to generate and package products or services.

Organizations may concentrate on highly flexible uses of production capabilities in a "job-shop" setting or may build on unique combinations of technical operations capabilities. In either case, products or services are often generated in relatively small numbers or are single projects unique to the customer. The features and benefits of the products or services will be set by the customer's specification and the nature of the organization's capabilities. Turnaround time and low costs are important competitive factors, particularly for a "job-shop" environment.

This type of organization will target markets selectively based on its particular mix of capabilities. Customers for new products or services may vary considerably from those of the core business.

The business priorities of an Operations Capability company generally follow this pattern:

1. Improve its position in current markets with its current products or services.

2. Offer additional products or services (based on its capabilities) to current markets.

3. Offer its product or services (based on its capabilities) to new markets.

    Example: Bechtel Group, Inc.

METHOD OF DISTRIBUTION/SALE

An organization pursuing a Method of Distribution/Sale Driving Force has a set or system of distribution and sales capabilities and the physical and human resources necessary to fully exploit them in order to provide a variety of products or services with a particular competitive advantage. These distribution and sales capabilities may be unique in their quality, quantity, or position compared with those of competitors. They may provide the organization with an opportunity to price its products at a premium. Alternatively, the organization may build on its ability to exploit distribution and sales capabilities similar to those of its competitors at a lower cost.

To gain maximum advantage from its existing distribution and sales capabilities or system, an organization may choose to handle compatible products which are not its own. The organization may also seek to develop or acquire other distribution or sales channels or systems which are similar in nature to its current capabilities. The specific content and scope of its capabilities may change over time so that the organization sustains a competitive advantage in its uniqueness or low-cost position.

The organization with a Method of Distribution/Sale Driving Force will target markets selectively, based on its particular mix of distribution and sales capabilities. Customers for new products or services may vary considerably from those for the original products, provided they can be reached through existing or similar distribution and sales channels/systems.

The business priorities of a Method of Distribution/Sale organization generally follow this pattern:

1. Improve its position in current markets with its current products by building on its uniqueness or low-cost position.

2. Through its distribution and sales capabilities offer new products to current markets.

    Example: Book-of-the-Month Club, Inc.

NATURAL RESOURCES

An organization pursuing a Natural Resources Driving Force owns or controls a significant natural resource (or more than one). It possesses the capability to process that natural resource into usable forms. The organization's competitive advantage rests in the quality, quantity, location, or form of the natural resources themselves. The organization will therefore seek to maintain its advantage in one or more of these areas, adding to the natural resource ownership or control as necessary. It may also seek ownership or control of other natural resources that may be used as substitutes.

A Natural Resources–driven organization may itself produce a variety of products or services from the resource, or may license or joint-venture product development and production to other organizations. It will seek to ensure that these products or applications have added value for the customer or end user. Regardless of the current way this organization converts that natural resource to products, its primary strategy is to control that resource for future exploitation.

The business priorities of a Natural Resources organization will generally follow this pattern:

1. Deeper penetration of current customer groups and geographies with existing and modified products.

2. Expansion to new customer groups and geographies.

3. Provision of new products based on the same or substitute natural resources.

Example: Shell Oil Company

Index

215

About the Authors

Benjamin B. Tregoe, Ph.D., is chairman and chief executive officer of Kepner-Tregoe, Inc., an organization based in Princeton, New Jersey, specializing in strategic and operational decision making. Dr. Tregoe has helped executives set the future strategy for their organizations in the United States, Canada, Latin America, and the Far East. He is a leading lecturer whose articles have appeared in business journals throughout the world, and is coauthor of *The Rational Manager,* a landmark book of management methodology, as well as *The New Rational Manager.* Dr. Tregoe is also coauthor, with John Zimmerman, of *Top Management Strategy.*

John W. Zimmerman is senior vice president and director of Kepner-Tregoe, Inc., which he joined in 1961. Over the last fifteen years he has specialized, along with Dr. Benjamin Tregoe, in the development of a pioneering approach to setting and implementing an organization's strategic direction. He has helped organizations around the world apply that approach. Mr. Zimmerman is coauthor of *Top Management Strategy.*

Ronald A. Smith, Ph.D., is director of research and development for Kepner-Tregoe's Strategy Group. His responsibilities include new conceptual research and design. Dr. Smith consults with a broad range of high-technology, industrial, and service organizations.

Peter M. Tobia, Ph.D., is vice president of Kepner-Tregoe, Inc. During his thirteen years with the company, he has served as vice president, marketing, and as director of new product development. Dr. Tobia has worked with a wide number of organizations in the United States and internationally in the areas of strategic and operational decision making.